Artifacts that Enlighten:
The Ordinary and the Unexpected

Linda Stone, Barbara J. Heath, and Patricia M. Samford, Editors

Society for Historical Archaeology

2020

J.W. Joseph, Annalies Corbin, and Benjamin Ford
SHA Special Publication Editors

Artifacts that Enlighten: The Ordinary and the Unexpected

Library of Congress Control Number: 2020937483

Compiled with an introduction by:
Linda Stone, Barbara J. Heath, and Patricia M. Samford

Book Design by:
Tasheon Chillous & Knic Pfost

J.W. Joseph, Annalies Corbin, and Benjamin Ford, SHA Special Publication Editors

Abstract

Most of the artifacts archaeologists uncover are utilitarian and mundane. However, artifacts are sometimes recovered that provide a surprising narrative or present an interpretive conundrum. The articles in this volume share eleven stories of artifacts that enlighten, presenting artifacts of varying types, locales, and periods with engaging stories that illuminate the ways in which historical archaeologists encounter and interpret the past through material things.

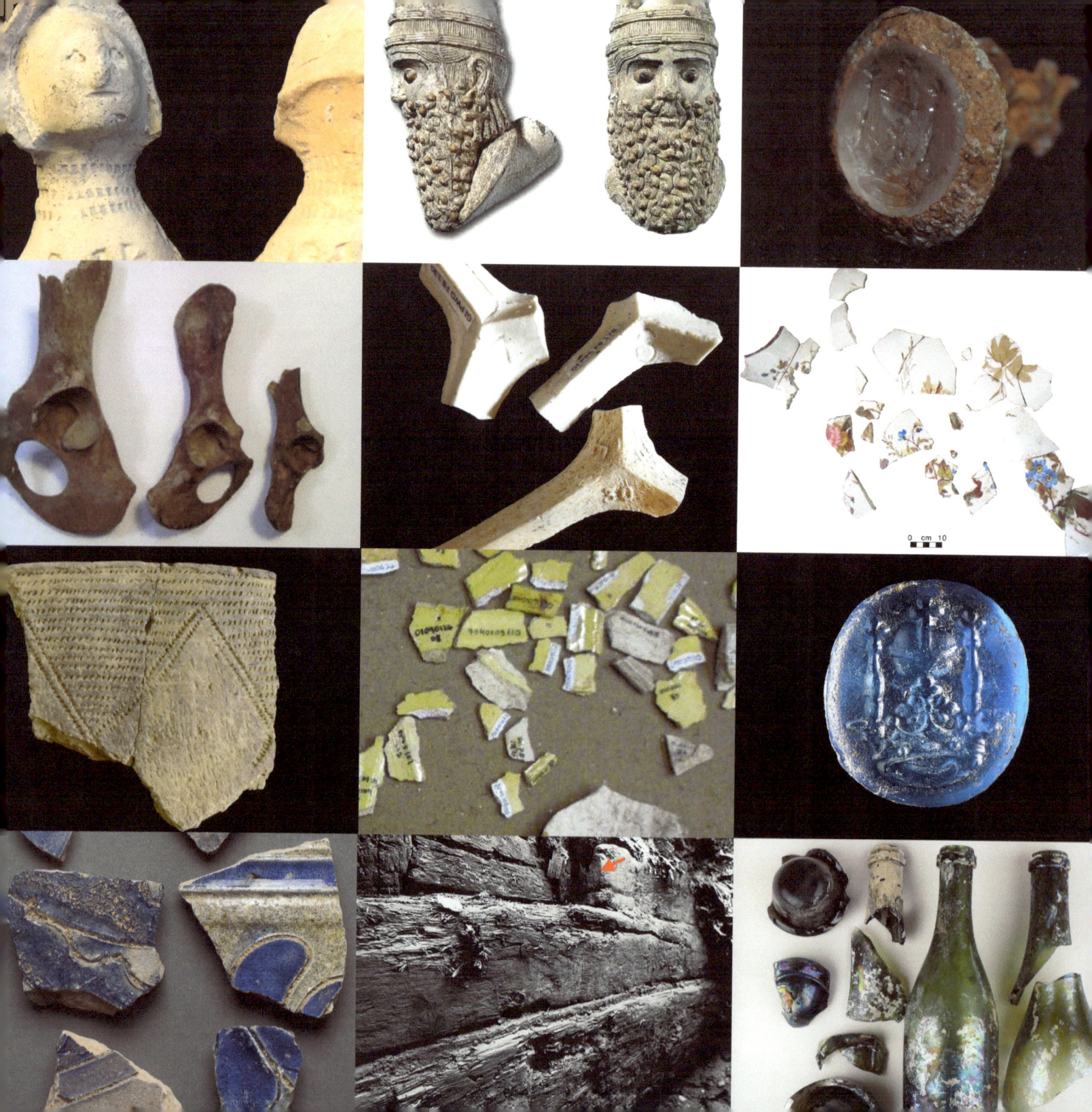

TABLE OF CONTENTS

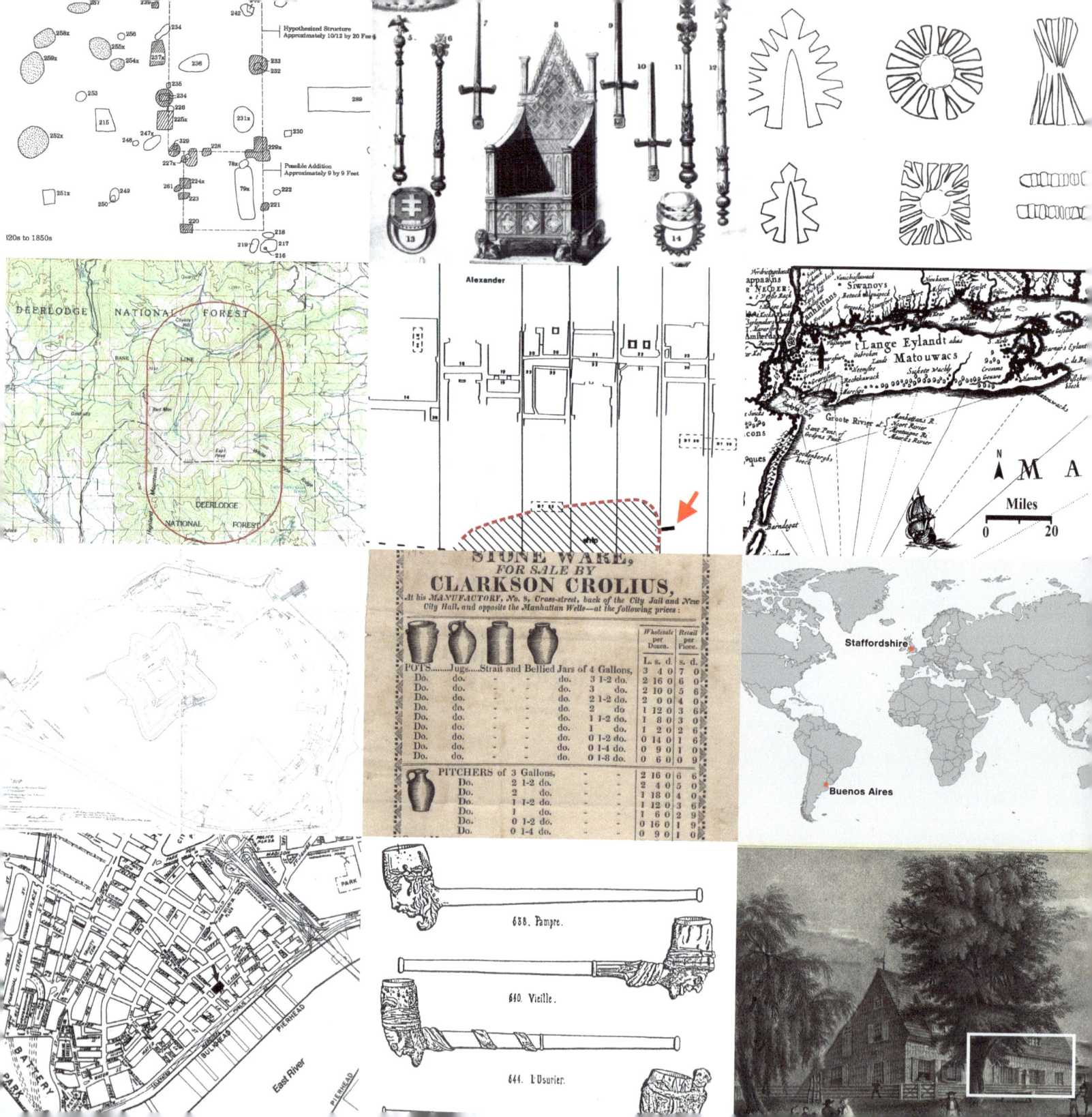

Introduction

Linda Stone

The majority of artifacts that historical archaeologists find are ordinary objects; things we recognize instantly and see frequently. However, every once in a while, one of these ordinary artifacts speaks to us. It could be because of the density of the find within a site, a unique motif it contains, its historical use, or because it just is not like the others of its type. Each of the chapters in this volume will present artifacts that are special, either because they are so ordinary or so unexpected and, perhaps, because they are a little of both.

These eleven chapters each present a special artifact. Artifacts include a tobacco pipe with a distinct motif and meaning in an antebellum, southern, free African American community (Joseph); a late-18th-century glass fob seal found at a slave quarter in Virginia (Heath); a mysterious earthenware form whose identification was a challenge (Samford); a champagne bottle found far from France (Victor); an unusually large collection of dog bones found at just one site (Pipes); a late-17th-century Dutch vessel identified at an English site that is hoped to bring greater awareness of this form (Schaefer); kiln stilts with unique embossing whose presence is a mystery (Stone); two locally-made tobacco pipe stems from different sites that exhibit shared decorative traditions (McMillan); German stoneware that was not imported from Germany (Janowitz); a Staffordshire jug found in South America (Guillermo and Majewski) and a brick that crossed the ocean (Geismar).

This volume was created as a result of the enthusiasm of participants and audience members who attended the 3-Minute Artifact Forum at the 2019 SHA Annual Conference in St. Charles, Missouri. The forum included fifteen presentations around the theme "Artifacts that Enlighten:

The Ordinary and the Unexpected." As archaeologists, we are accustomed to being unphased by material objects. However, sometimes we secretly do get excited by certain artifacts we encounter. It was the desire to share this excitement that led to the creation of the conference forum, and it was that excitement that snowballed into the creation of this volume.

The session organizer and co-editor of this publication would like to gratefully acknowledge the encouragement of Rebecca Allen and Alasdair Brooks, both prior 3-minute session organizers, for paving the way. Gratitude also goes to SHA executive director Karen Hutchison who provided advice on how to navigate the intricate, mysterious complexities of conftool, the conference registration system. This task was facilitated with the help of the extremely patient Steven Dasovich, the 2019 SHA conference chair, who personally had to override conftool more than once. Many thanks must also go to all of the session presenters who generated the enthusiasm that motivated us to turn the session papers into this publication and to those presenters who were ultimately available to participate in this publication. Thanks also go to Annalies Corbin, SHA co-publications chair, and to J. W. Joseph, SHA POD editor, for agreeing to take on this project. Finally, enormous thanks to my co-editors Barbara J. Heath and Patricia M. Samford who have made it possible for me to take on the task of turning a session into a publication, a first for me. I couldn't have imagined a better support team.

A Clay Pipe from Springfield:
Symbol and Meaning in an Antebellum Southern Free African American Community

J.W. Joseph

An object draws meaning from a variety of sources: material, form, function, period, design, style, decoration, and cost. Historical archaeology adds context as another layer of meaning. This essay explores a single object and the meaning gained from its archaeological context.

The object is an anthropomorphic clay tobacco pipe (Figure 1). Featuring a bearded male, decorations on the pipe bowl include bronze painted eyes, bronze painted beads braided into the beard, and large gold gilt Christian cross earrings. Two decorative headbands, studded with bronze beads, encircle the figure's forehead. The eyes and eyebrows were painted black. This pipe was made in a mold: two parallel seams extend along the sides of the pipe, while a third seam is seen at the rear center of the pipe bowl. The style of decoration would have required the pipe to be fired in bisque, then painted and fired a second time (Walker 1977). While the bowl is intact, the stem is broken off near the bowl.

Formed of white ball clay, the pipe is well made and appears to be of 19th-century origin with a higher than standard value due to the manufacturing process. The figure appears to be of Middle Eastern origins, which aids in its identification as the product of French pipe manufacturer Gambier. The Gambier pipe manufactory was in business from 1780 to 1926; this particular design appears in an undated Gambier catalog *Nomenclature des Pipes Gambier* (V Hasslauer & De Champeaux [1855]:46), where it is identified as the "Ninevien" design (Figure 2). While the catalog does not contain a publication date, the late Michael Pfieffer (1991, pers. comm.) indicates that anthropomorphic pipes gained popularity in the 1850s, which suggests it is from this period, as do other artifacts from the pit feature where it was found.

The clay pipe was recovered from a household in the Springfield community (Joseph 1991, 2008). Springfield was a free African American community established on what were then the outskirts of Augusta, Georgia in the years following the Revolutionary War. African Americans who had gained their freedom during the Revolution flocked

FIGURE 1. Anthropomorphic tobacco pipe from a pit feature associated with the Springfield community (Photograph by the author, 1991).

to the community, which provided opportunities for their employment through the river trade, as craftspeople in a growing town, and in domestic service. Laws of the period prohibited African Americans from owning property, and the household from which the pipe was recovered appears to be a squatter residence of vernacular construction using salvaged materials (Figure 3). This house was found on the flood-prone banks of the Savannah River in an area that was not developed until the 1870s. The pipe bowl was recovered from a pit feature associated with this dwelling, which also contained a transfer-printed vessel dating to the 1850s.

The Springfield community was anchored by religion, and oral history of the community states that services began around a spring in a field. This religious gathering was formalized as the Springfield Baptist Church in either 1787 (Cashin 1980:65, 1995; Anderson 1987:4) or 1793 (Brooks 1922:190–191; Raboteau 1986: 210). Springfield Baptist

Church continues operations as the nation's oldest continually operating African American church.

As an expression of status by an African American resident of Springfield, the ownership and use of this pipe would have flown in the face of Augusta city ordinances of the time. Historian Edward Cashin (1980:63) notes than an 1802 August City Council ordinance prohibited free and enslaved African Americans from smoking a pipe or cigar in public; the ordinance stated that such "privileges" should be reserved for whites. Haughton (1972:16) cites a similar ordinance in Savannah during the 1850s, and observes, "the mere act of smoking in public by a Negro might bring a penalty of two dollars, three dollars, eight lashes or thirty lashes." Joyce (1992) and Johnson and Roark (1984) note that there was growing tension between the races over the use of items reflecting higher social status, and class, by African Americans.

All of this evidence points to this clay pipe as a socially charged artifact. Used in the context of the free African American Springfield community, the pipe denoted the user as a person of social standing, and the Biblical imagery of the pipe may have represented an association between its owner and the Springfield Baptist Church. If used on the streets of Augusta, within the view of whites, the pipe would have served as a challenge to white domination and as an expression of a free African American's social and economic achievements and standing.

However, the significance of this artifact may extend beyond this preliminary reading of social context. Archaeological excavations at what was thought to be Nineveh (the site was later identified as the town of Nimrod) were conducted in the 1840s by Austen Henry Layard. Layard published his findings in 1849 as *Nineveh and Its Remains* (Layard 1849). Within this volume, Layard illustrated the discovery of a large statue that shares attributes of the pipe's design, including the braided hair and beard (Figure 4). It is conceivable that this illustration served as the basis of Gambier's design, and

it is almost certain that the pipe was produced following the publication of Layard's book.

Layard's excavations laid the foundations of the field of Biblical Archaeology, which was then in its infancy. The archaeological discovery and excavations of a place depicted in the Bible were taken, at that time, as proof of the Bible's veracity. This discovery fueled the Christian resurgence that had begun in the 1830s and that led to the "Third Great Awakening" of 1857. It is thus possible that these archaeological excavations may have been a topic of sermons at the Springfield Baptist Church, and that free African Americans may have seen in this archaeological work the proof of

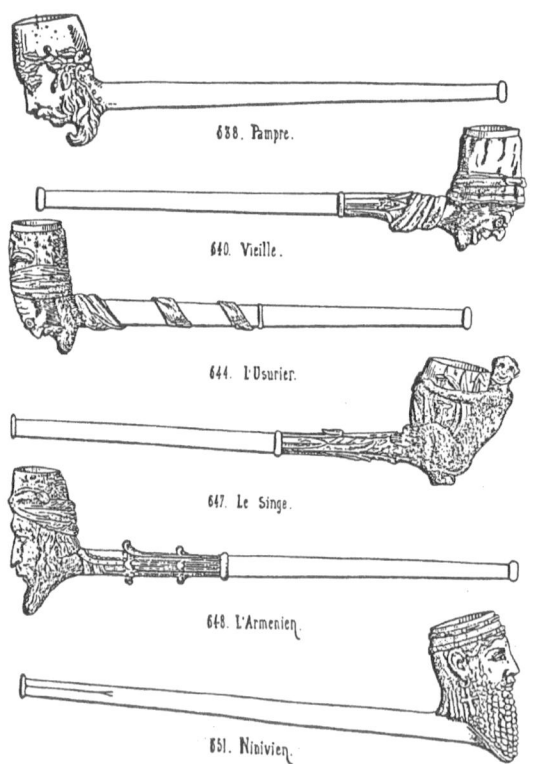

FIGURE 2. French pipe manufacturer Gambier catalog showing example Number 651, Ninevien (Nomenclature Des Pipes Gambier, [1852]).

J.W. Joseph

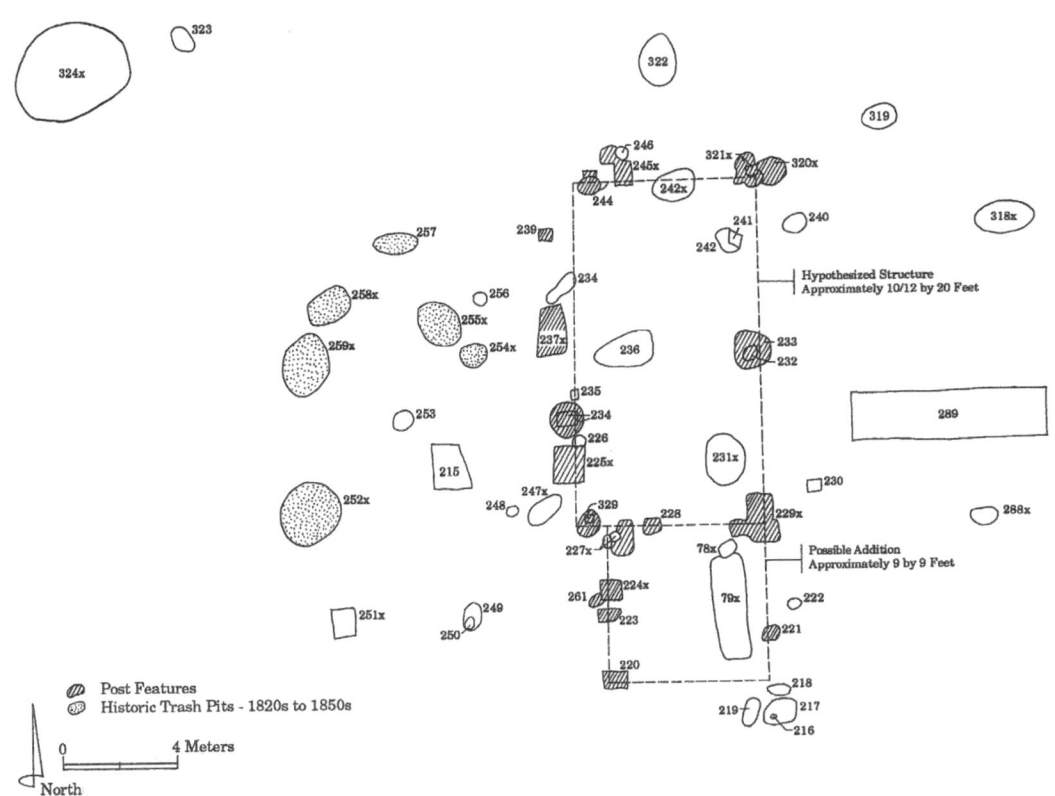

FIGURE 3. Springfield excavation plan showing interpreted structure plan and surrounding pit features, including feature 254, which produced the tobacco pipe (Drawing by New South Associates, 1991).

Discovery of the Gigantic Head.

FIGURE 4. Illustration from *Nineveh and Its Remains*, showing discovery of statuary head that may have influenced Gambier's pipe design (Layard 1849).

Nineveh's existence, as well as proof of events depicted in the Bible and a promise of the future.

Biblically, the Ninevites were depicted as a free-spending and wicked people who were also slaveholders. The Old Testament Prophecy of Nahum tells of God's destruction of the town, and more significantly, of God's freeing of its slaves (New English Bible 1970:1136–1137):

These are the words of the LORD:

Now I will break his yoke from your necks
and snap the cords that bind you.
Image and idol will I hew down in the house of
your God.

This is what the LORD has ordained for you;
never again will your offspring be scattered;

The recovery of the Ninevite pipe from the free African American Springfield community carries multiple levels of meaning. Ownership of this pipe might have symbolized Christian belief in a community built around the Springfield Baptist Church. However, use of this decorative pipe in a public setting would have been a violation of municipal laws and a challenge to white authority. The pipe's owner, and their compatriots, might also have seen hope for a better future, for the end of slavery, in this pipe, as depicted in the Old Testament whose physical legacy had recently been archaeologically confirmed. Biblical Archaeology may have given the citizens of Springfield and their cohorts hope for the future. Historical archaeology provides the context for this pipe that allows its full meaning and symbolism to be interpreted.

J.W. JOSEPH

New South Associates, Inc.

6150 East Ponce de Leon Avenue

Stone Mountain, GA 30083, USA

References

Anderson, Betty
1987 *Springfield Baptist Church: A Church History*. Published by Springfield Baptist Church, Augusta, GA.

Brooks, Walter H.
1922 The Priority of the Silver Bluff Church and its Promoters. *Journal of Negro History* VII(1):172–195.

Cashin, Edward
1980 *The Story of Augusta*. Richmond County Board of Education, Augusta, GA.

V Hasslauer & De Champeaux
[1855] Nomenclature des Pipes Gambier. A Givet, Adrenenes/

Haughton, Richard H.
1972 Law and Order in Savannah, 1850–1860. *Georgia Historical Quarterly* LVI(3–4).

Johnson, Michael P., and James L. Roark
1984 *No Chariot Let Down: Charleston's Free People of Color on the Eve of the Civil War*. W. W. Norton & Company, New York, NY.

Joseph, J.W.
1991 *"And They Went Down Both Into the Water:" Archaeological Data Recovery of the Riverfront Augusta Site (9Ri165)*. Report to the City of Augusta, GA, from New South Associates, Stone Mountain, GA.

2008 Springfield: An Archaeological History of a Free African-American Community from the Revolution to the Civil War. *Early Archaeology* 36(1):79–96.

Joyce, Dee Dee
1992 Race, Class, Gender, and Ethnicity: An Analysis of Social Relations in Antebellum Charleston, South Carolina. Paper presented at the 1992 Annual Meeting of the Society for Historical Archaeology, Kingston, Jamaica.

Layard, Austen Henry
1849 *Nineveh and Its Remains: With an Account of a Visit to the Chaldears Christians of Kurdistan and the Yesidis, on Devil Worshipping, and an Inquiry into the Manners and Arts of the Ancient Assyrians*. G. P. Putnam, New York, NY.

New English Bible, with the Aprocyrpha
1970 Oxford University Press and Cambridge University Press. Oxford, U.K.

Nomenclature Des Pipes Gambier
[1852] Hasslauer & De Champeaux, Design 651, Ninevien.

Raboteau, Albert J.
1986 The Slave Church in the Era of the American Revolution. *In Slavery and Freedom in the Age of the American Revolution*, Ira Berlin and Ronald Hoffman, editors, p. 193–216. University of Illinois Press, Chicago.

Walker, Ian C.
1977 Clay Pipes with Particular Reference to the Bristol Industry. *History and Archaeology*, Number 11. National Historic Parks and Sites Branch, Parks Canada, Ottawa.

Revolutionary Change?

Barbara J. Heath

Mounted seals descended from signet rings, pieces of jewelry with designs embedded within the ring's face. Members of the upper classes, mostly men, used these objects to identify themselves through initials or symbolic devices pressed in wax on legal documents, and business and personal correspondence. Signets were generally made of precious or semi-precious stones, and mounted in silver or gold. By the 18th century, seals with looped attachments that were worn on the body, but not necessarily on the finger, had begun to replace rings (Fales 1995:18–20). When fob watches came into style in the early 19th century, jewelers began to attach seals to watch chains or chatelaines, and these objects became known as fob seals (Fales 1995:128–129; Beal 2008:157).

A seal within a copper alloy mount of a style popular in the second half of the 18th century was uncovered at Wingos, a quarter farm within the Poplar Forest plantation in Bedford County, Virginia (Figures 1 and 2). It was found in plow zone above a subfloor pit associated with a circa 1770s–1780s slave quarter (Figure 3). The seal is made of colorless glass measuring 13 × 16 mm, with the complete object measuring 18 × 22 mm (Figure 4). An intaglio with an identical design was found at Cardiff University in Wales and donated to the National Museum of Wales in 1924. Unfortunately, this object has no other context information associated with it. It is made of blue glass, is unmounted, and is almost the same size as the intaglio associated with the Virginia seal, measuring 15 × 13 mm. Although catalogued as "(?) 14th cent." (Williams 1993:27), the object is now believed to be of post-medieval origin based on the Wingos' find (Chapman 2019, pers. comm.) (Figure 5).

I have not yet been able to pinpoint the original purpose of the seals; but the iconography on the objects provides some important clues. The intaglios contain a series of symbols relating to British nobility. The coronets on both seals consist of a trefoil leaf in the center, two small spikes, and the sides of two additional leaves, indicating that a crest coronet is depicted in both (Child 1965:98). Immediately above the coronet is a symbol, known as the "orb and crown," or "Sovereign's orb" which takes the form of a golden ball, and has historically

FIGURE 1. View of copper alloy mount and glass seal (Photograph by author, 2011).

represented the global power of the monarch and the rule of Christianity. On either side of the orb, extending down to the top of the coronet, are two scepters. The level of detail on the intaglios is much simplified; however, the top of both scepters appears to represent the dove with outstretched wings, one of two scepters historically carried by British monarchs (Figure 6, Thomson 1820:85,88).

Although laden with symbols of power, the Virginia seal was made of fairly inexpensive materials. Glass substituted for the more standard practice of using semi-precious or precious jewels, and copper alloy took the place of silver or gold. The seal was likely manufactured as an affordable accouterment of public office, and distributed to serve public and official, rather than personal and private, business. Both John Wayles, who owned Poplar Forest until his death in 1773, and Thomas Jefferson—who married Wayles' daughter, inherited the property, and established Wingos in an attempt to clear his father-in-law's debts—served as representatives of the Crown in public office. Wayles was King's Attorney for Charles City and Chesterfield Counties in the mid-18th century and Jefferson served as a member of the colonial legislature (Charles City County Order Book 1737–1751:265,

FIGURE 2. View of seal face and mount (Photograph by author, 2011).

280, 386, 455, 485, 518–521; Chesterfield County Court Order Book 1, 1749–1754:412).

Why such a seal with royal symbolism was present at Wingos is a mystery. John Wayles likely fathered six children with the enslaved woman Betty Hemmings. Two of their enslaved daughters, Doll and Mary, lived at Wingos briefly in the early 1770s. Thomas Jefferson spent time at Poplar Forest, including the Wingos quarter, during the American Revolution. Either of these men may have given the seal away once royal symbols no longer carried power in Virginia. Alternately, one of the enslaved residents of the site might have appropriated it, or Jefferson might have lost or discarded it. This latter scenario seems unlikely given the seal's proximity to the subfloor pit—it appears to have been disturbed from that sealed context by later plowing. The fob seal's new association with the household of an enslaved person or persons, dating to the years of, or immediately following, the American Revolution, supports the idea that it took on a significantly different meaning at this time. The old seal's presence within a quarter attests to the object's radical change in meaning immediately following the American Revolution—although what that new meaning became remains unknown.

In 1776, while Jefferson was in office, Virginia declared its independence from the crown and designed a new state seal. A variant of the new seal can be seen on a pewter medallion, struck in 1780, to be given to Indian allies during the American Revolution (Figure 7). Like the medallion, the seal depicted a scene containing the Roman goddess Virtus, dressed as an Amazon, holding a sword and spear. Beneath her feet lay the body of George III (later stylized as Tyranny), his crown fallen, his chains broken, clutching a scourge (Evans 1911:31; Adams 1992:128–132; Tarter 2014).

Unfortunately, the end of tyranny proclaimed by the motto of the new state seal did not extend to the enslaved residents of Poplar Forest. It would be another 87 years before the chains of slavery were broken in Virginia.

Acknowledgments

I thank Laura and Gene Goley for permission to conduct research on their property and their interest in this project; and the students and volunteers who assisted in the excavations at Wingos, especially Eleanor Breen, Daniel Brock, Suzanne Johnson, Lauren McMillan, Crystal Ptacek O'Connor, and Hope Smith. I am also grateful for the financial support of the National Endowment for the Humanities, and the Department of Anthropology and the Office of Research at the University of Tennessee. Thanks to Lynsey Bates, formerly of the Digital Archaeological Archive of Comparative Slavery, who found the intaglio at the National Museum of Wales and shared her research with me, and to the staff of the British Museum and the National Museum of Wales for their help in obtaining images. A complete catalogue of artifacts, contexts, and features, along with maps, images, and bibliographic references for Wingos can be found at www.daacs.org.

Barbara J. Heath

FIGURE 3. View of Wingos slave quarter (44BE0298) with two subfloor pits. The seal was found in plow zone sealing the pit to the right (Photograph by author, 2009).

FIGURE 4. Seal face showing crown, orb, and scepters (Photograph by author, 2011).

Barbara J. Heath

FIGURE 5. Intaglio, blue glass. National Museum of Wales, Accession Number 24.520
(©Amgueddfa Genedlaethol Cymru, ©National Museum of Wales, 2019).

FIGURE 6. Royal symbols of power (Thomson 1820, plate IV).

FIGURE 7. Pewter medallion, "Happy While United," minted 1780 (© The Trustees of the British Museum, 2019).

BARBARA J. HEATH

Department of Anthropology
University of Tennessee
1621 Cumberland Ave.
Strong Hall Room 502A
Knoxville, TN 37996, USA

References

Adams, John W.
1992 The Virginia Happy While United Medal. *American Journal of Numismatics* 3/4:123–134.

Beal, Peter
2008 *A Dictionary of English Manuscript Terminology, 1450-2000.* Oxford University Press, Oxford, UK.

Charles City County Order Book
1737–1751 Charles City County Order Book. Microfilm Reel 14. Library of Virginia, Richmond.

Chesterfield County Order Book
1749–1754 Chesterfield County Order Book 1. Microfilm Reel 38. Library of Virginia, Richmond.

Child, Heather
1965 *Heraldic Design, A Handbook for Students.* G. Bell and Sons, London, UK.

Evans, Edward S.
1911 *The Seals of Virginia.* Virginia State Library, Richmond, VA.

Fales, Martha Gandy
1995 *Jewelry in America, 1600–1900.* Antique Collectors' Club. Woodbridge, UK.

Tarter, Brent
2014 Seal of the Commonwealth of Virginia. *Encyclopedia Virginia.* Virginia Foundation for the Humanities <https://www.encyclopediavirginia.org/seal_of_the_commonwealth_of_virginia#start_entryWeb>. Accessed 12 September 2019.

Thomson, Richard, editor
1820 *A Faithful Account of the Processions and Ceremonies of the Kings and Queens of England; exemplified by that of their most Sacred Majesties King George the Third and Queen Charlotte: with all the other interesting proceedings connected with that magnificent festival.* John Major, London, UK.

Williams, David H.
1993 *Catalogue of Seals in the National Museum of Wales.* Vol. I, Seal Dies, Welch Seals, Papal Bullae. National Museum of Wales, Cardiff.

Porringer, Pan or Pipe Stand?

Parsing an Unusual 17th-Century Earthenware

Patricia M. Samford

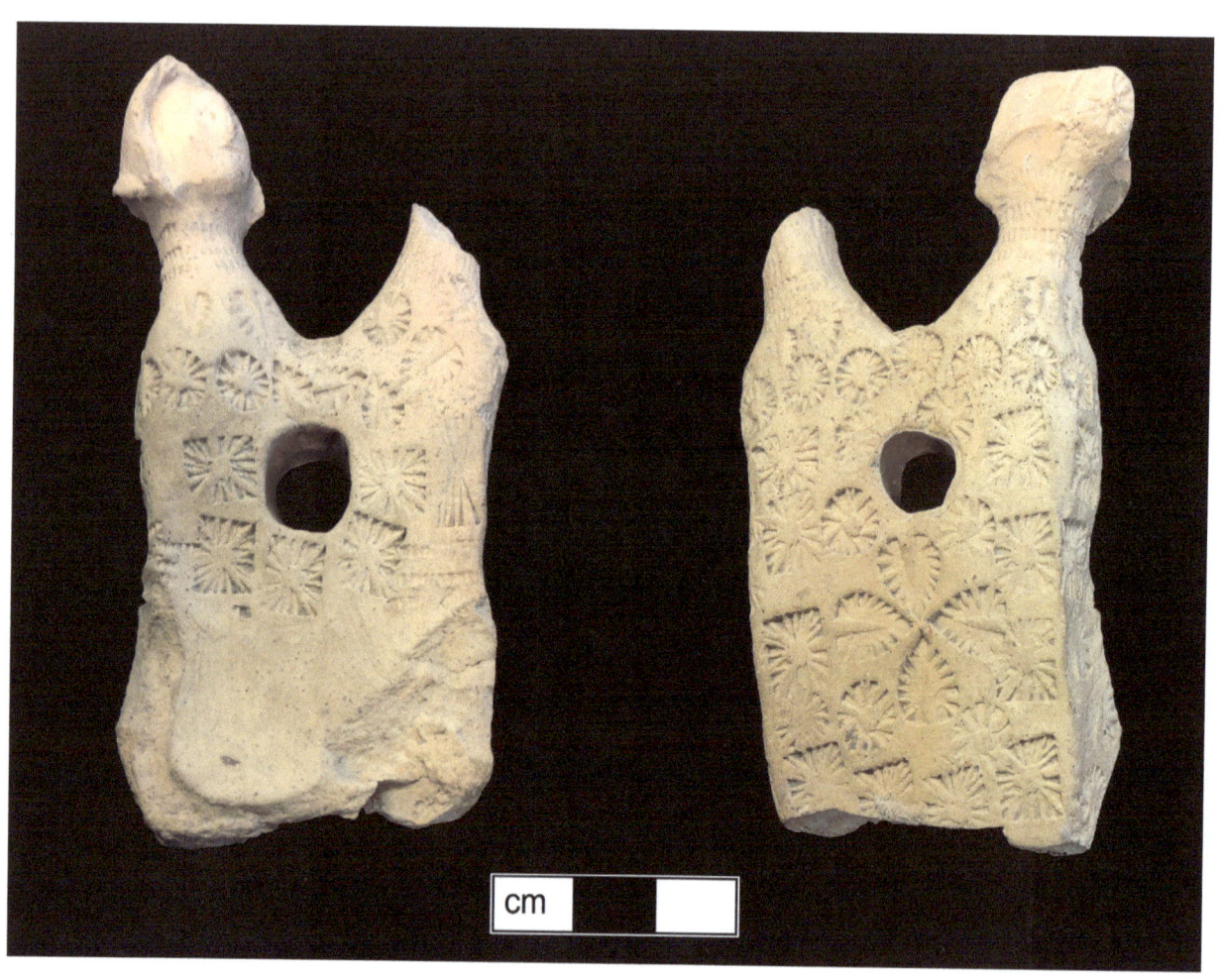

Salvage archaeological excavations took place in 1990 on the Eastern Shore of Maryland at the site of "My Lord's Gift" (18QU30), the home of wealthy planter and attorney Henry Coursey (Custer et al. 2019). The excavation revealed a cruciform-shaped main house and an earthfast kitchen, both occupied during the second half of the 17th century, as well as a number of refuse pits and fence lines. An unusual ceramic figural object was recovered from a refuse pit dated to the third quarter of the 17th century (Figure 1).

Two human figures diverge from the base of this 9 cm tall object, whose bottom edge has been broken away. The intact figure represents a female, as evidenced by her 17th-century style Dutch cap head covering (Bradfield 1987). The shaping of the head, while not incredibly detailed, is skillfully handled and the face bears simple, but pleasing features (Figure 2). The other figure, presumed to be a male, is missing its head. The remainder of the artifact is covered with rouletting and stamped motifs (Figure 3). Comparative paste analysis, plus x-ray fluorescence testing, point to the artifact being locally-made, not English or European (Custer 2018).

Extensive research and consultation with scholars of 17th-century material culture did not result in any definitive conclusions about the function of this unusual artifact. Three possible functions are offered here: a tobacco pipe stand, a spit support, and a handle to a cooking-related vessel like a porringer, chafing dish, or dripping pan. The evidence supporting each idea is discussed and a conclusion based on the best evidence is offered.

Pipe Stand: Based on the similarity of the stamped decorations to ones used on 17th-century locally-made tobacco pipes in the Chesapeake (Luckenbach and Cox 2002; Luckenbach and Kiser 2006), one hypothesis was that the object functioned as an accoutrement used in smoking. Two of the figure's impressed stamps are identical to those used on a locally- made tobacco pipe stem recovered from the Coursey Site (Figure 4). A possible explanation would be its use as a stand for holding pipes. The central hole or the notched shoulder area could have held upright the stem and bowl of a lit pipe when the smoker had a task that required the use of both hands. While feasible, no evidence has yet been discovered for the existence of 17th-century pipe stands. Although pipes and smoking accoutrements—tobacco boxes, tapers and braziers—were common in 17th-century Flemish and Dutch paintings, no pipe stands were depicted. The 1647 painting "Still Life with Pipe" by Dutch painter Pieter Claesz shows a lit tobacco pipe perched precariously against a bundle of tapers, while other similarly dated Dutch paintings depict comparable scenes of pipes propped against braziers, plates, or loaves of bread. The earliest stands in the online collections of the Amsterdam Pipe Museum date from the 1800s, so it appears that this form of material culture did not exist in the 17th century.

Spit Support: Alternately, this object may have been part of a set of wedge-shaped pottery spit supports, similar to examples documented in the Netherlands and in 17th- and early-18th-century England (Grigsby 2000). A rod holding a joint of meat would be suspended through the holes of two supports and used in conjunction with an earthenware dripping pan placed underneath the roasting meat to catch juices for making sauces and gravies.

The spit support interpretation is interesting for several reasons. The Coursey artifact is broken at its base, suggesting the missing portion could have added enough height and stability to this object to make it functional as a spit support for small cuts of meat or fowl. Also, many of the European spit supports illustrated in Heidinga and Smink (1982) were highly decorated with wheels, lozenges, stars, triangles, or circles, including examples with three-dimensional human and animal heads (Figure 5). While the latest European examples date at least a century earlier than the Coursey site, potters in England's North Devon district made spit supports

FIGURE 1 (opposite page). Front and rear views of earthenware figural artifact (Photograph by author, 2019).

FIGURE 2. Detail of female figure's head, front and back (Photograph by author, 2019).

and other hearth furniture in the 17th and early-18th centuries (Cramp 2015).

Ceramic Vessel Handle: It is also possible this object was the handle to a hollow vessel used for food preparation or consumption, like a porringer or posset pot. The shape of the Coursey object is similar to flat handles seen on chafing dishes, skillets, and braziers made in England from 1550 to 1700. A more likely possibility is that the object was part of a dripping pan whose two vertical handles incorporated slots and holes for spit supports, hence combining the dripping pan and roasting apparatus in one vessel.

Interpretation: The evidence presented here points towards this artifact being part of a dripping pan with vertical handles incorporating a spit support, as shown in Kent (2014) (Figure 6). Evidence from the Netherlands indicates the similarity of this artifact's overall shape, appearance, and decorative elements to fired clay spit supports from the 13th to the 16th centuries (Heidinga and Smink 1982). The Coursey artifact likely represents a vertical handle to a dripping pan, rather than a freestanding spit support. This object may not be robust enough to have been a free-standing spit jack and a slightly concave undecorated area at the lower

Patricia M. Samford

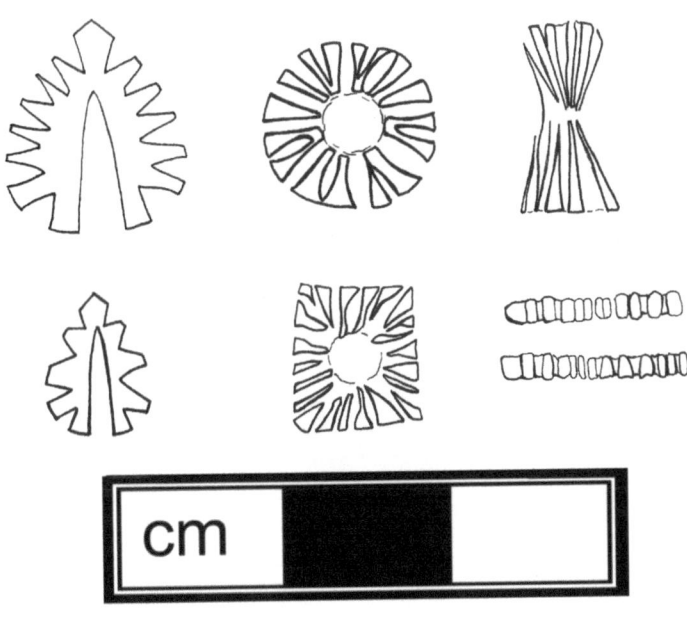

FIGURE 3. Stamped elements on the Coursey earthenware object (Drawing by Alex Glass, 2016).

front of the object suggests instead that it was part of a hollow vessel similar to the vertically-handled dripping pan.

The presence of decorations on all sides of the object also suggests a vertical, rather than a horizontally-placed handle. The exuberant display of leaves and sunbursts and especially the four-leaf clover on the object's reverse side were meant to be seen. Decorations on the reverse of a horizontally-placed handle would not have been visible. Additionally, there would be no need for a hole in a horizontally-placed handle.

No artifacts comparable to this object have yet been found in the Chesapeake. Was this object a one-of-a-kind piece, perhaps commemorating the marriage of Henry Coursey to Mary Harris in 1658 (Papenfuse et al. 2010:236) or his second marriage to Elizabeth Morgan after 1670? The female and presumably male figures could represent the newly married couple, with the four-leaf clover iconography bringing forth wishes for faith, hope, love, and luck. If it does represent a locally produced piece, as the material testing suggests, it was possibly made by Morgan Jones, Maryland's first recorded potter, in operation from 1661 to 1691 (Chappell 1975; Kelso and Chappell 1975). Some of Jones' vessels were decorated with impressed sunburst marks like those used on this figure (Figure 7).

Perhaps further research into the archaeology of post-medieval England and Northern Europe may reveal additional

FIGURE 4. Decorated local pipe from Coursey Site (Photograph by Jay Custer, 2018).

Patricia M. Samford

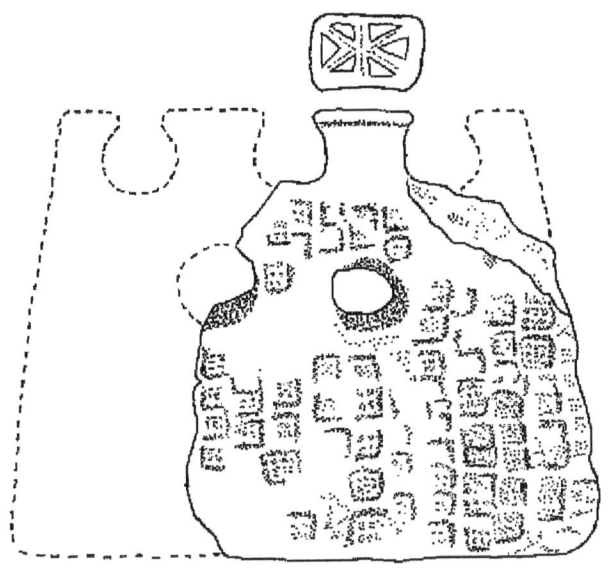

Inches

FIGURE 5. Fired clay spit support from Netherlands (Drawn by Patricia Samford from Heidinga and Smink, 1982).

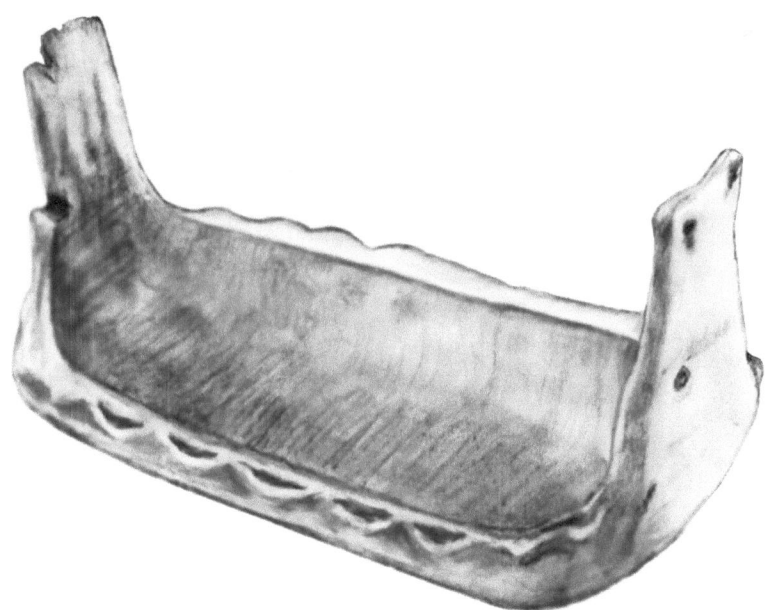

FIGURE 6. Dripping pan with spit supports built into the vertical handles. From the Netherlands, circa 1400 to 1500. Vessel height: 18.5 cm and vessel length: 32 cm (Drawn by Sharon Raftery from http://collectie.boijmans.nl/ed/object/49277, 2016).

Porringer, Pan or Pipe Stand

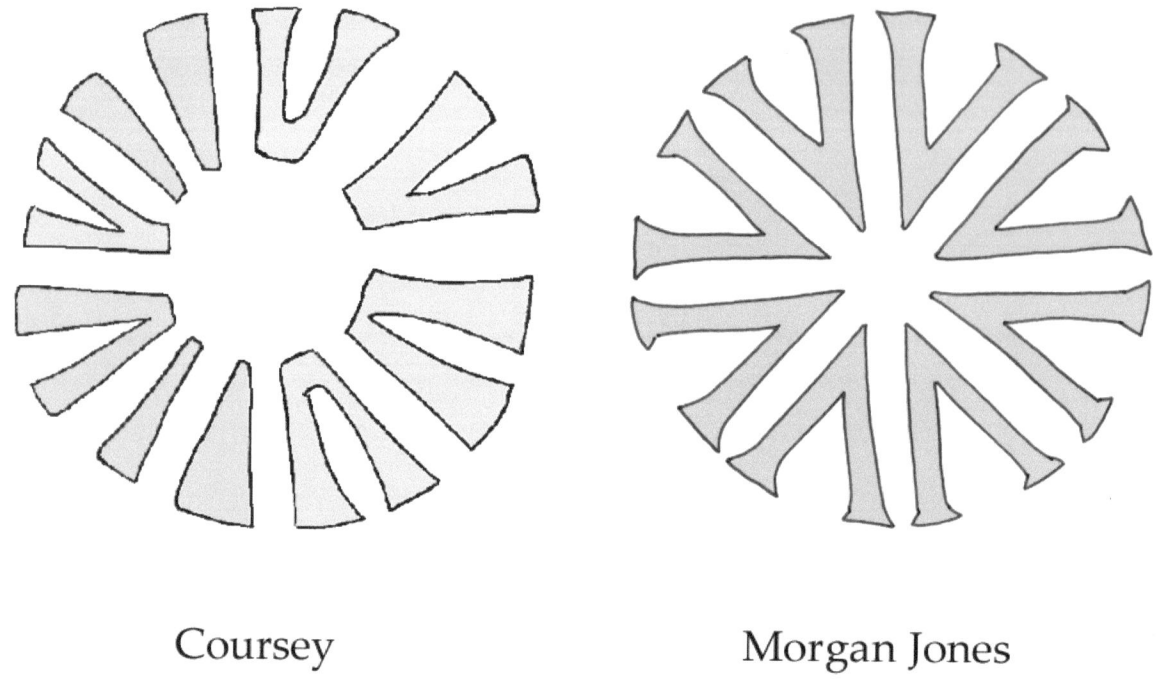

Coursey   Morgan Jones

FIGURE 7. Stamped marks from potter Morgan Jones and Coursey object. Not to scale (Drawing by Alex Glass, 2016).

evidence, but until then, there will always be mystery around this intriguing artifact.

Acknowledgments

The preparation of this article benefited from the expertise of a number of supportive colleagues, to whom I offer many thanks. They include Bly Straube of the Jamestown-Yorktown Foundation for the spit support suggestion and reference, Taft Kiser of Stantec, Inc. for information on local pipe manufacturers, and Robert Hunter of the Chipstone Foundation for his thoughts on the function of the artifact and for suggesting other scholars I could query. Jay Custer of the University of Delaware commented on various iterations of this article, provided background information on the site and offered a number of useful ideas that have been incorporated into this article. I would also like to thank David Higgins and Peter J. Hammond of the Society for Clay Pipe Research, John Allan, and Don Duco of the Amsterdam Pipe Museum. My colleagues at the Maryland Archaeological Conservation Laboratory—Ed Chaney, Rebecca Morehouse and Sara Rivers Cofield—offered ideas and comments during the long process of research and writing. Other MAC Lab staff members were also instrumental in the preparation of this article; Alex Glass prepared the illustration of the stamped motifs and Sharon Raftery drew Figure 6. Randy Larsen, St. Mary's College of Maryland, conducted the x-ray fluorescence study and Julia A. King, also of St. Mary's College of Maryland, discussed this artifact with me on numerous occasions.

Patricia M. Samford

PATRICIA M. SAMFORD

Maryland Archaeological Conservation Laboratory
Jefferson Patterson Park and Museum
10515 Mackall Road
St. Leonard, MD 20685, USA

References

Bradfield, Nancy
1987 *900 Years of English Costume; From the Eleventh to the Twentieth Century.* Crescent Books, New York, NY. First published in 1938.

Cramp, Cynthia
2015 North Devon Relief-Decorated Ceramics in the Household. *In West Country Households, 1500–1700,* pp. 189–221. The Society for Post-Medieval Archaeology Monograph 9. The Boydell Press, Woodbridge, UK.

Chappell, Edward A.
1975 Morgan Jones and Dennis White: Country Potters in Seventeenth-Century Virginia. *Virginia Cavalcade,* Spring 1975:149–155.

Custer, Jay F.
2018 Comparative Analysis of Paste and Design Elements of Earthenware Figurine from 18QU30 – "My Lord's Gift", A 17th-Century Colonial Habitation Site, Queen Ann County, Maryland. University of Delaware Center for Archaeological Research Report No. 6. Newark, DE.

Custer, Jay F., Andrea Anderson and Nedda Moqtaderi
2019 "Halcyon Days" on the Eastern Shore of Maryland: Current Research at "My Lord's Gift" (18QU30), the 17th and 18th Century Home of Henry Coursey and His Family. *Maryland Archeology* 52(1&2):1–8.

Grigsby, Leslie B.
2000 *The Longridge Collection of English Slipware and Delftware.* Jonathan Horne Publications, London, UK.

Heidinga, H. A. and E. H. Smink
1982 Brick Spit-supports in the Netherlands (13th–16th Century). *Rotterdam Papers IV:* 63–82.

Kelso, William M. and Edward A. Chappell
1974 Excavation of a Seventeenth Century Pottery Kiln at Glebe Harbor, Westmoreland County, Virginia. *Historical Archaeology* 8:53–63.

Kent, Oliver
2014 English Country Pottery—Dripping Pans, Bacon and Apple Roasters. *Clay and Fire* <https://drojkent.wordpress.com/2014/05/20/english-country-pottery-dripping-pans-bacon-and-apple-roasters/>. Accessed 28 January 2016.

Luckenbach, Al and C. Jane Cox
2002a Tobacco-Pipe Manufacturing in Early Maryland: The Swan Cove Site (ca. 1660–1669). *In The Clay Tobacco-Pipe in Anne Arundel County, Maryland (1650–1730),* Al Luckenbach, C. Jane Cox and John Kille, editors, pp. 46–63. Anne Arundel County's Lost Town Project, Annapolis, MD.

Luckenbach, Al and Taft Kiser
2006 Seventeenth-Century Tobacco Pipe Manufacturing in the Chesapeake Region: A Preliminary Delineation of Makers and Their Styles. *In Ceramics in America 2006,* Robert Hunter, editor, pp. 161–177. Chipstone Foundation, Milwaukee, WI.

Papenfuse, Edward C., Alan F. Day, David W. Jordan and Gregory A. Stiverson
2010 *A Biographical Dictionary of the Maryland Legislature 1635–1789.* Johns Hopkins University Press, Baltimore, MD.

International Tastes In Gold Town

Megan Rhodes Victor

Continuing the theme for this collection of "artifacts that enlighten," the object at the heart of this chapter represents the unexpected – or even extraordinary – among the ordinary: a bottle for expensive imported French champagne that had made a 9,000-mile journey to the remote high desert gold-mining town of Highland City in western Montana. The presence of alcohol in a 19th-century mining town is not unexpected; however, finding French champagne among American beer and bitters bottles in a frontier saloon at about 10,000 feet in elevation was an unanticipated part of the Highland City excavations.

Highland City (24SB67) sprang up around the gold-rich Fish Creek, which twisted through the Highland Mountains in what is today southwestern Montana. Three prospectors – J.B.S. Coleman, E.B. "Egg" Coleman, and William Crawford – found gold there on 25 July 1866 while panning in the creek. Later that summer, a second group of prospectors, William Owsley, Tom Hall, and Franck Beck—reportedly extracted gold worth about $3,100 in a single day. The gold ore at Highland City quickly gained attention for its purity, selling at $20 per ounce, while ores from nearby Butte, near the base of the Highland Mountain ridge, only commanded $16 per ounce (Anaconda Standard 1899a; Sahinen 1935; Lyden 1948; Wolle 1962; Wilde 1999; Montana DEQ 2013; Victor 2018). Adding to the young town's wealth, gold ran not only in Fish Creek, but also through a dry gulch, named Cooley's Gulch, that sat just below Highland City. Soon, the towns of Highland City and Red Mountain City merged as a two-town conglomeration that stretched for about ten miles (Wolle 1962; Wilde 1999; Montana DEQ 2013; Victor 2018) (Figure 1).

Prospectors found gold-bearing lode ores almost immediately after finding placer gold and had located at least 100 different lodes after only three years (Wolle 1962; Victor 2018). Two months after the first discovery of gold in the District, the population of Highland City numbered roughly 600 people. During the height of the town's boom, from 1868 to 1872, the population is estimated to have been at least 2,000 and it may have reached 5,000 individuals. While never specified, these estimates likely refer to the conglomeration of Highland City and Red Mountain City rather than Highland City alone. This population made the conglomeration the largest settlement in Southern Deer Lodge County, which at the time included present-day Silver Bow County and the town of Butte, Montana, and stretched up to the Canadian border. To put the population into perspective, the total population of Montana Territory in 1870 was 20,000 people, which meant that approximately one tenth of the entire Territory's population (or as much as a quarter of the population, if using the estimate of 5,000 individuals) resided at Highland City-Red Mountain City (Anaconda Standard 1899b; Davis 1962; Wolle 1962; Victor 2018; U.S. Census Bureau 1901).

Overall, the prospectors and miners recovered roughly $2.3 million in gold from the Highland Mining District surrounding the two-town conglomeration from 1866 to the mid-1890s. At its height, Highland City had 300 wooden houses and cabins, 5 dance halls, 10 saloons, several general stores, and a cemetery. The town also garnered enough attention within Deer Lodge County that it had its own stop on the post route, along a road called the Highland Trail, which ran from Alder Gulch to the Highland Mountains.

The presence of just shy of a dozen saloons in Highland City speaks to one of the key ways that the residents chose to spend their time – and their money. The bottles recovered from these saloons attest to the kinds of alcohol that residents chose to buy. Archaeological excavations, conducted at the site in 2013, 2014, and 2016, located at least one of these ten saloons, including a rich alcohol-related assemblage. Through a combination of pedestrian survey, shovel test pit survey (with shovel tests placed at 10 m intervals), and a 1 × 1 m test unit, a minimum of 60 glass vessels were recovered from the saloon assemblage, 28 of which was collected from the test unit.

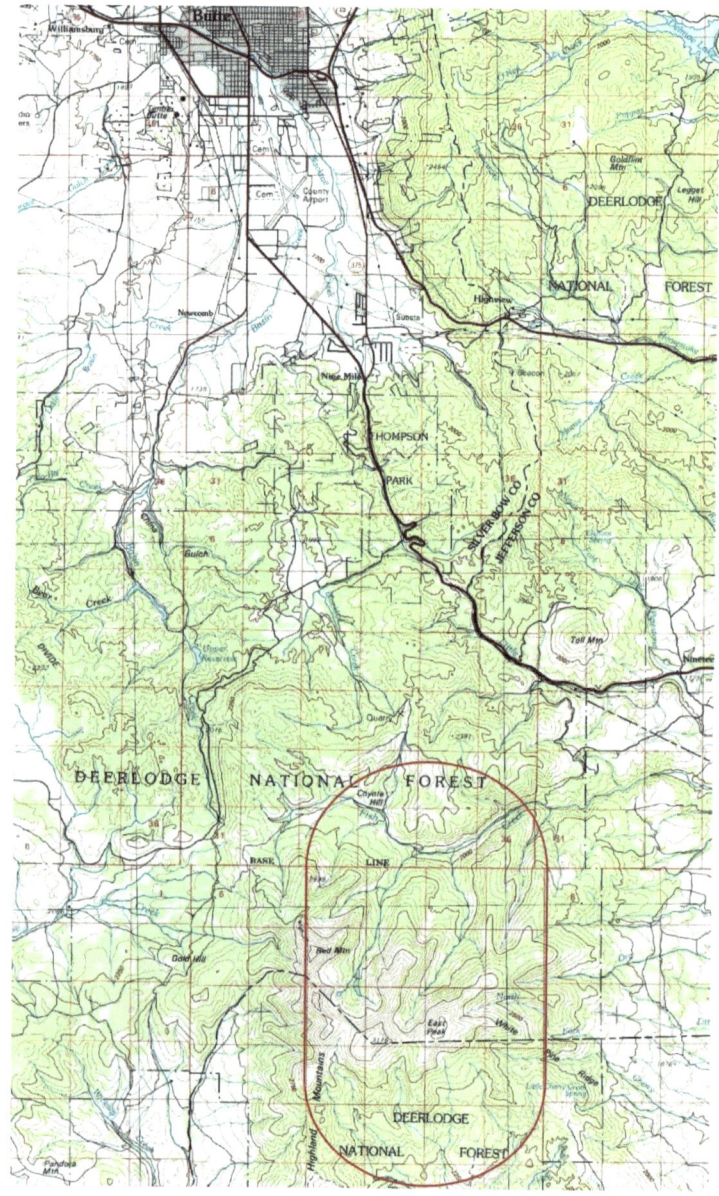

FIGURE 1. USGS 1990 Butte South, MT 1:100,000 Scale Topographical Map Showing Approximate Location of Highland City, Montana (Exact Location Protected by USFS).

The saloon assemblage yielded at least one Kelly's Log Cabin Bitters bottle, manufactured in St. Louis, Missouri; one P.H. Drake Sazerac bottle, manufactured in New York, New York; a union clasped hands flask, likely from Philadelphia; and at least four champagne bottles, including two whole vessels (Figure 2). These olive green bottles all came from the same area of the site and have the same narrow shape, pronounced kick-up, or punt, and a champagne finish (Lindsey 2010). Several of the bottle sherds (and both whole bottles) had fragments of foil still attached to the neck, just below the finish. Found near these bottles, on the same transect, was a fragment of foil embossed with "H. RI[?]…Co. / RHEIMS."

The French town of Reims is known today as one of the country's centers for producing champagne. It rose to prominence as a center of wine production from the 1860s to the 1880s, when the entire Champagne region shifted its wine-making focus to more urban markets (Guy 2007). During the third quarter of the 19th century, and the early part of the last quarter of that century, the Champagne region experienced a period of financial prosperity and the price of grapes rose steadily, particularly from the 1870s to the 1880. In some regions, it increased by over 100% in a decade (Guy 2007). This price was transferred to the sparkling wines as well, along with costs for transporting the bottles from the region to cities and to the coast.

The presence of champagne at Highland City, which was occupied during this prosperous period for the Champagne region's winemakers—in which the price of grapes and bottles of Champagne rose—indicates that the residents chose to buy a particularly expensive alcohol, especially when compared with the bitters found in the same saloon deposit. The mining town's remote location added further costs to the purchase price of the champagne bottles, which covered a distance of over 9,000 miles from Reims to Highland City. The bottles had to be transported from the mountainous vineyards just south of Reims to the city itself, and then to a nearby

FIGURE 2. French Champagne Bottle and Bottle Fragments Recovered from Highland City (Photograph by author, 2018).

port, likely Calais. From there, they were shipped across the Atlantic to merchants on the East Coast of the United States, sent to Saint Louis, and then carried along the Missouri River to Three Forks, Montana. The final leg of the trip was by coach to the base of the Highland Mountain range about 60 miles away, and – at last – in an ox-cart up another 2,000 feet in elevation to Highland City. The champagne bottles at Highland City were likely as much of an unexpected delight to visitors of the town as they were to the archaeologists who uncovered them.

Megan Rhodes Victor

MEGAN RHODES VICTOR

Stanford Archaeology Center
Stanford University
488 Escondido Mall, Building 500
Stanford, CA 94305, USA

References

Anaconda Standard
   1889a *Chronicling America: Historic American Newspapers. 06 January.* Library of Congress <https://chroniclingamerica.loc.gov/lccn/sn84036012/1899-01-06/ed-1/seq-4/>. Accessed 12 August 2019.

   1889b *Chronicling America: Historic American Newspapers. 05 September.* Library of Congress <https://chroniclingamerica.loc.gov/lccn/sn84036012/1899-09-05/ed-1/seq-6/>. Accessed 12 August 2019.

Davis, Jean
   1963 *Shallow Diggin's, Tales from Montana's Ghost Towns.* Caxton Printers, Caldwell, ID.

Guy, Kolleen M.
   2007 *When Champagne Became French: Wine and the Making of a National Identity.* The Johns Hopkins University Studies in Historical and Political Science (Book 121). Johns Hopkins University Press, Baltimore, MD.

Lindsey, Bill
   2010 Bottle Typing / Diagnostic Shapes Dating. In *Historic Glass Bottle Identification & Information Website* <https://sha.org/bottle/wine.htm#Champagne%20Bottles>. Accessed 15 September 2019.

Lyden, Charles J.
   1948 *The Gold Placers of Montana.* Montana Bureau of Mines and Geology, Memoir No. 26. Montana School of Mines, Butte.

Montana Department of Environmental Quality (DEQ)
   2013 Historical Context, aka Fish Creek. In *Historical Narratives.* Montana Department of Environmental Quality, Abandoned Mine Lands <https://deq.mt.gov/Land/AbandonedMines/linkdocs/187tech>. Accessed 15 August 2019.

Sahinen, Uuno M.
   1935 Mining Districts of Montana. Masters Thesis, Montana School of Mines, The Montana College of Mineral Sciences and Technology, Butte, MT.

United States Census Bureau
   1901 Bulletin 33. Population of Montana by Counties and Minor Civil Divisions. *Twelfth Census of the United States.* U.S. Department of Commerce, U.S Census Bureau, Washington, DC.

Victor, Megan Rhodes
   2018 On the Table and Under It: Social Negotiation & Drinking Spaces in Frontier Resource Extraction Communities. Doctoral Dissertation, Department of Anthropology, the College of William & Mary, Williamsburg, VA.

Wilde, James D.
   1999 Highland City (111-217) In *A Plan for the Management of Historic Mines in Montana: Placer & Hardrock, Compiled by Josef J. Warhank.* The Montana State Historic Preservation Office, Helena, MT.

Wolle, Muriel Sibell
   1963 *Montana Pay Dirt: A Guide to the Mining Camps of the Treasure State.* Sage, Denver, CO.

Philly Dogs

Marie-Lorraine Pipes

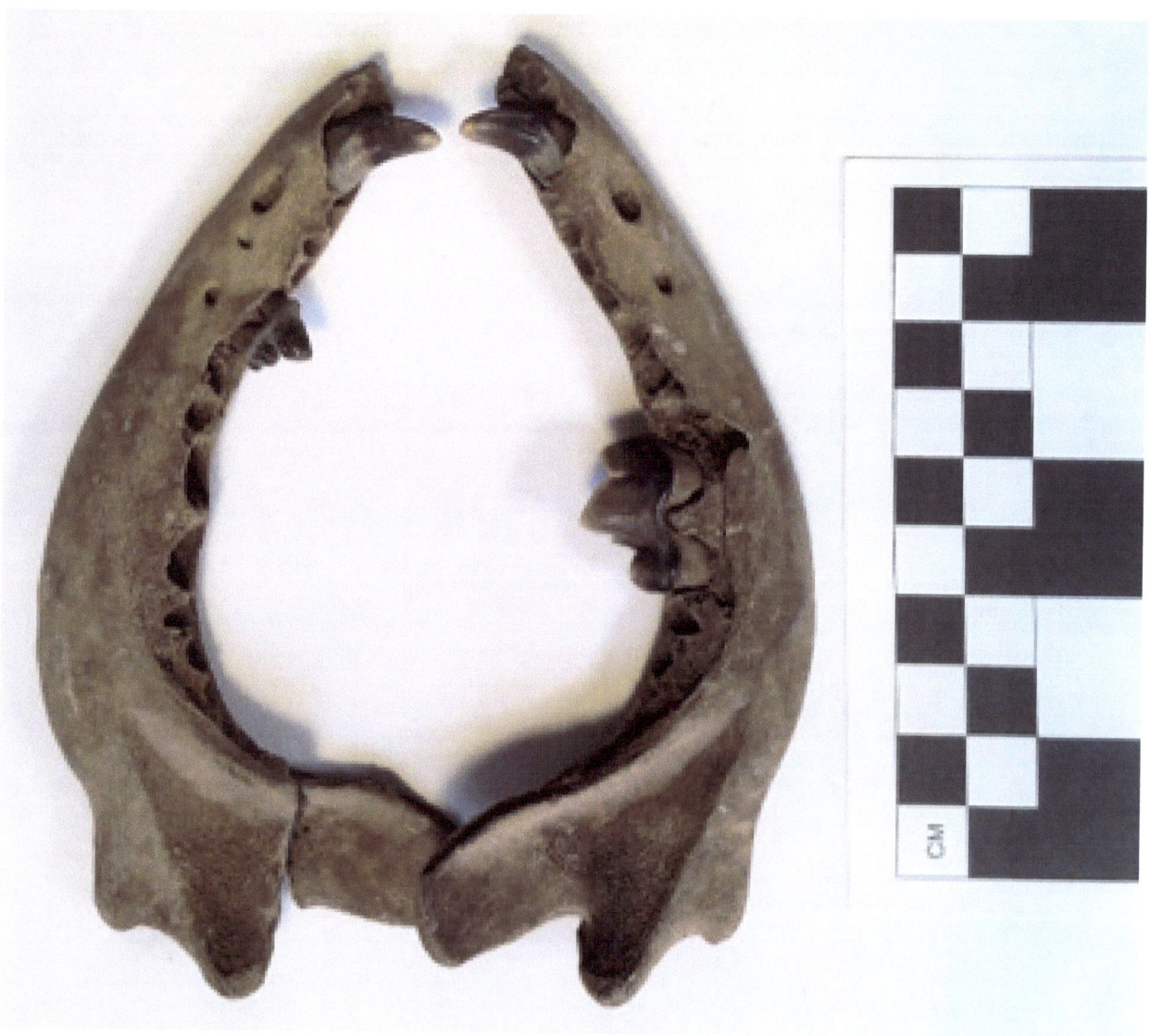

Excavations at the National Constitution Center Site uncovered a backyard feature containing a large concentration of dogs. While cats are commonly found archaeologically, dogs are rarely found on urban sites. They are generally buried, not thrown in trash deposits, and treated with greater respect than other species. The analysis revealed a very high frequency of immature animals, long-term accumulation of dogs, a number of dog breeds, and dissection of dog carcasses. The results of the analysis, combined with documentary research, suggest that the deposit was generated by a dog catcher.

The National Constitution Center Site (NCC) is in the historic district of Independence Mall of Philadelphia. The National Constitution Center, the National Park Service, and AECOM collaborated in the study of the NCC faunal assemblage. The NCC site yielded one of the largest faunal assemblages ever recovered from Philadelphia, estimated at 350,000 bone specimens. Aside from dogs, it is composed of a great range of mammals, birds, fish, and turtles obtained from feature and backyard deposits. Comparatively speaking, these deposits are highly repetitive and extremely diverse in species composition and refuse types.

Occupation of the site started in the late 18th century when Philadelphia was poised to become one of the greatest cities in the United States. The colonial city sat between two rivers, bordered by highly productive agricultural lands and was famous for markets offering a vast array of animal and plant-based foods. Its rapid expansion in size and population resulted in increasing challenges to the legal, social and economic infrastructures, which included dog regulations.

Feature 191 was a large brick shaft feature containing 105 dogs, which were distributed throughout 10 strata indicating a long-term accumulation. Many dog skeletal elements were coated in lime added to accelerate decomposition of carcasses though some limb bones still had fur (Figure 1). Dog remains were found in two other deposits: Feature 124 had one dog, and Feature 148 had four dogs. In Feature 191, age groups

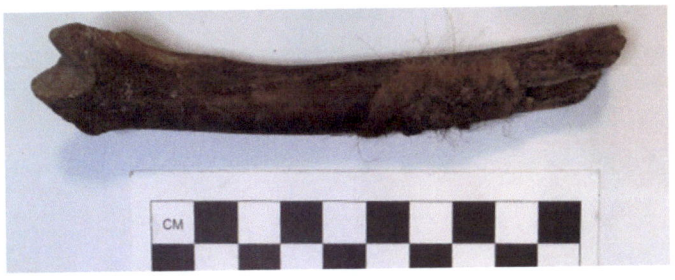

FIGURE 1. Immature dog femur with brown fur attached (Photograph by author, 2017).

included fetuses, neonates, juveniles, subadults, adults and seniors (Table 1). Most of the dogs in all three features were neonates and juveniles when they died, whereas seniors were least common (Figure 2). High frequencies of fetuses reveal the presence of pregnant female dogs. The high rate of immature animals is abnormal, suggesting that dogs were selected for by cultural agents.

Comparison of size and stature of specific skeletal elements across age groups indicated that distinct breeds were represented. The most obvious breed was a bulldog, indicated by a robust, curved set of mandibles from an adult (Figure 3) (Stewart Thomson 1996). In comparison, the mandibles from a neonatal puppy, likely a hound, are larger and less curved (Figure 4). Based on the large size and developmental age of these mandibles, the puppy, had it survived, would have grown quite large. Many skeletal elements of the same developmental ages varied in size, further revealing the presence of distinct breeds, as can be seen by innominates from three adults (Figure 5). These individuals would have been noticeably different in size. Stature was considered when comparing skeletal elements of the same developmental age and size. Some dogs were robust, while others were gracile.

The analysis looked for cause of death and state of health. Most of the dogs appeared to be in good health, though some suffered from cancers, anemia, and arthritis. One individual had a nail driven through the cranium, another

Feature/Stratum	Fetus	Neonate	Juvenile	Subadult	Adult	Senior	MNI
124	-	1	-	-	-	-	1
148.5	-	1	-	-	1	-	2
148.7	-	1	1	-	-	-	2
191.1-2	1	1	-	-	1	-	3
191.3	2	2	-	-	1	-	5
191.4	2	5	7	2	1	-	17
191.5	2	6	9	2	3	3	19
191.6	1	7	4	1	3	-	16
191.7	1	4	6	-	1	-	12
191.8	-	5	1	1	1	-	8
191.9	2	7	1	2	1	-	13
191.10	1	3	-	1	1	-	7
Total MNI	12	43	29	9	14	3	110

TABLE 1. Minimum Number of Individuals (MNI) By Age Group.

was shot with a small caliber bullet. One dog may have been dissected, with the presence of butcher marks suggesting removal of limb bones.

This unusual collection of dogs begs explanation. Like humans, late-18th-century dogs lived socially-situated lives in Philadelphia. Their status varied according to the identity of their owners. As dog numbers increased in urban areas, many problems arose concerning ownership and control (Hall 2017). Dogs were not allowed to roam the streets as they were legally constrained and managed by their owners.

There are countless advertisements and articles concerning dogs and their owners in the *Pennsylvania Gazette*, as well many other Gazettes, dating from the 18th and 19th centuries. These accounts describe romantic stories, pet illnesses and remedies, animal dissections, and commentaries on the traits of dog breeds. They describe feats of bravery,

signs of intelligence, and acts of cruelty involving attacks on other animals and humans. They also include legal notices of taxation, of lost and missing dogs, and offers of rewards for their return.

In the late-18th century, stray dogs with pedigrees were valuable, as they were status symbols of the elite (Meacham 2011). Owners put notices in newspapers offering financial rewards both for their recovery, and in cases of theft, information about the thieves (Breig 2004). Dogs were also considered dangerous because of aggressive behaviors and illnesses, especially rabies. An untrained dog was a potential threat to society, so owners had to train and control their dogs (Wagner 2014). Dog rabies became an issue and purges occurred to drive populations down (Howard-Smith 2018).

Dogs' dependency on humans for food, especially in urban settings, was a growing concern in the 18th century.

Marie-Lorraine Pipes

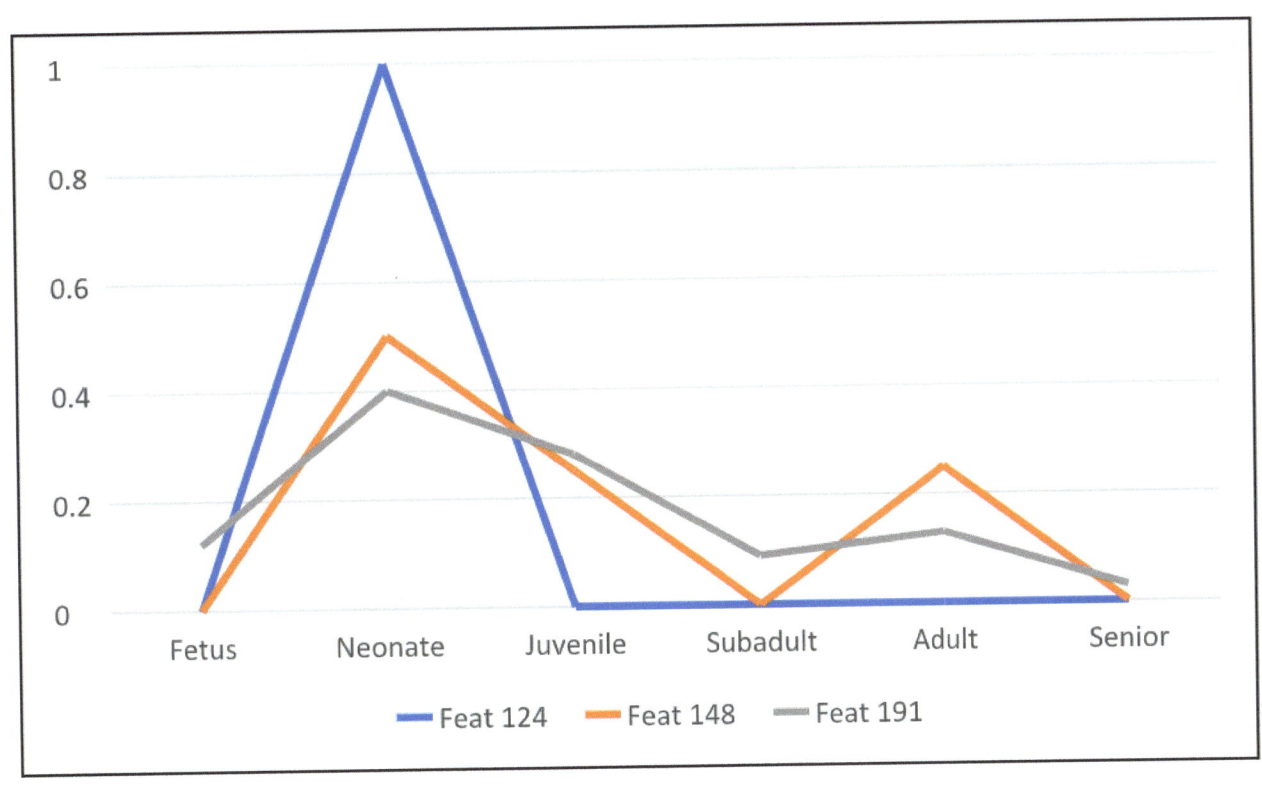

FIGURE 2. Age group distributions, relative percent based on Minimum Number of Individuals (Graph by author, 2017).

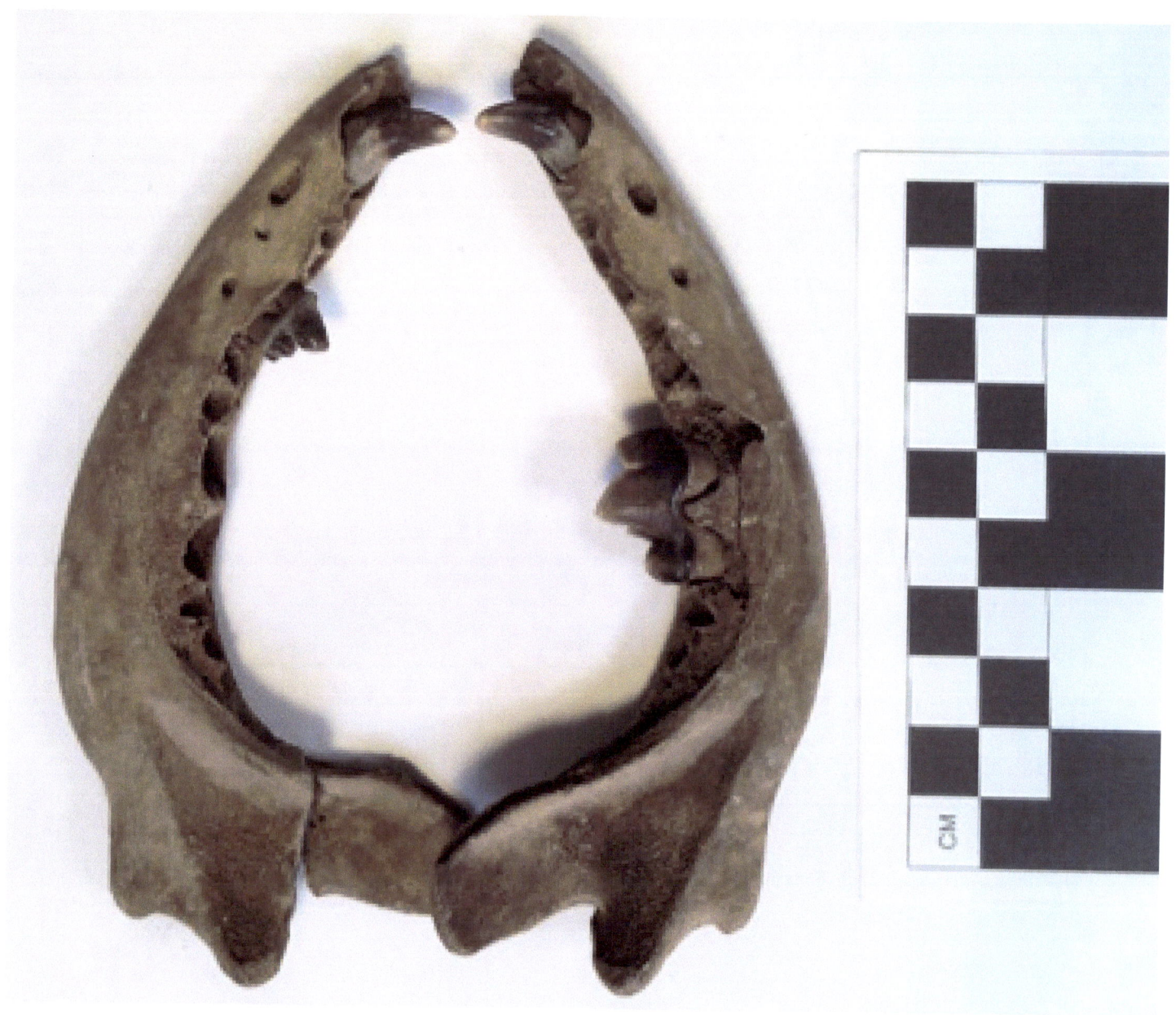

FIGURE 3. Set of adult bulldog mandibles (Photograph by author, 2017).

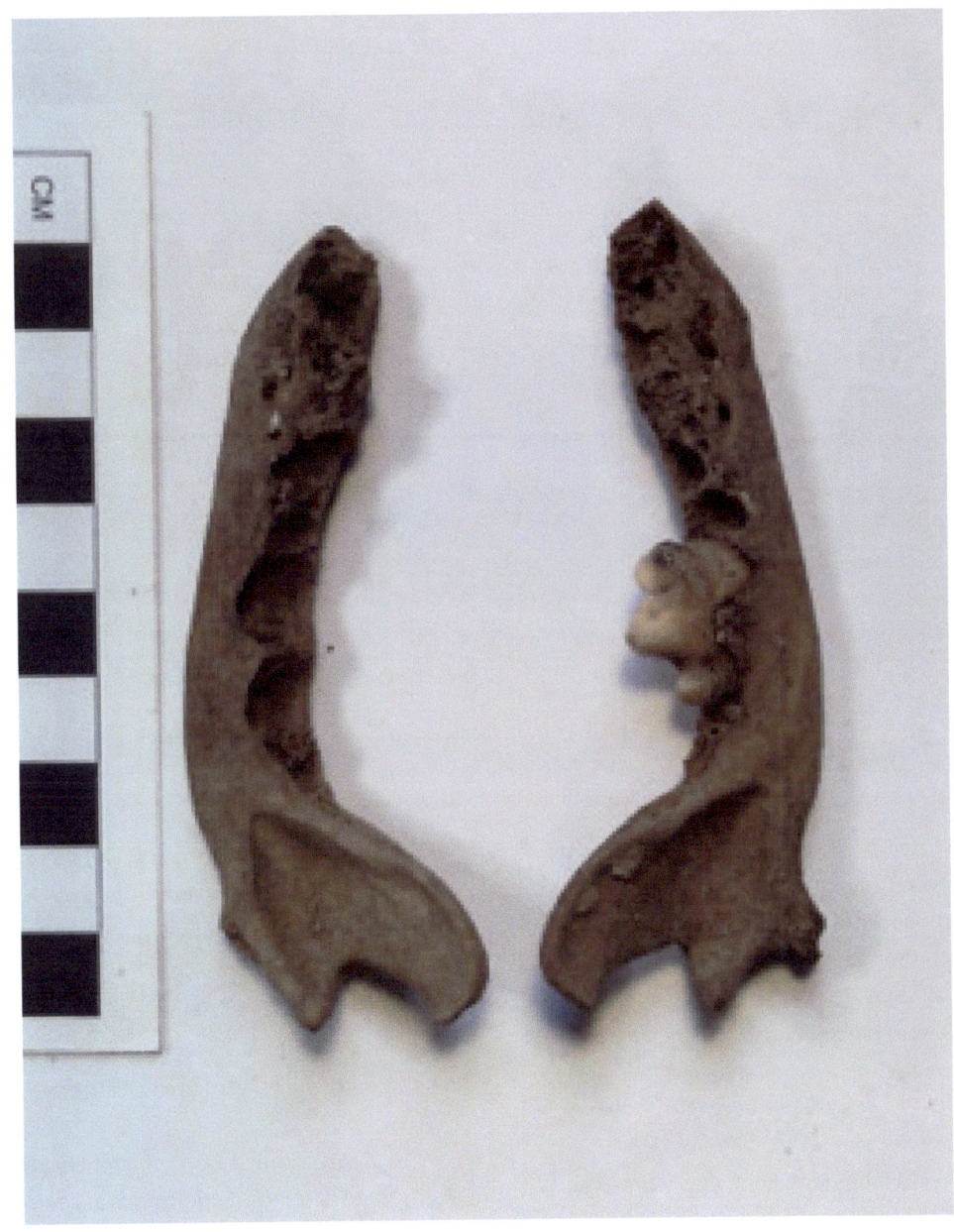

FIGURE 4. Set of immature hound robust mandibles (Photograph, by author 2017).

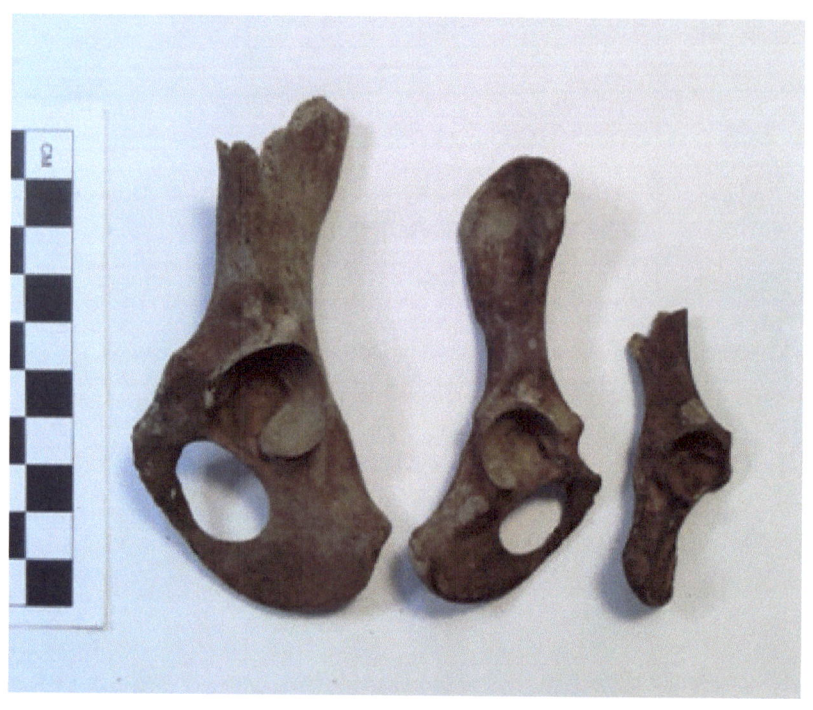

FIGURE 5. Innominates from three adult dogs of different breeds
(Photograph by author, 2017).

Major cities in England struggled to provision their citizenry when the Industrial Revolution resulted in the movement of masses of rural people seeking work in factories, often bringing their dogs with them. Complaints were filed about the food requirements of dogs because they competed with those of humans. Laws were passed limiting one dog per household as well as taxing dog owners on an annual basis (Tague 2008; Murden 2019). Dogs without collars, or whose owners who failed to pay the annual tax, were put down. Similar laws were passed in America as dog populations and problems increased (Wang 2012).

Owners had to train, feed, and restrain dogs and pay the annual fee. Unless living outside the city, or wealthy, most people could only afford one dog per household. It seems probable that an agent such as a dog catcher was responsible for generating the Feature 191 dog assemblage. Whoever created the deposit served the city by destroying unwanted puppies, pregnant females, elderly and sick individuals, and stray and aggressive dogs. This case study may explain why it is rare to find dogs archxaeologically in urban deposits.

Acknowledgements

My thanks to Jed Levin, Chief Historian, Independence National Historical Park, for his support and guidance in this research. I also thank AECOM for the opportunity to work on the NCC project. I am grateful to Meta Janowitz for her constructive comments. And last but not least, thank you to Linda Stone for encouraging me to experience the intensity and challenge of a three-minute presentation.

MARIE-LORRAINE PIPES

Zooarchaeologist, Consultant
SUNY Geneseo College and AECOM Inc.
323 County Road 9
Victor, NY 14564, USA

References

Breig, James
2004 The Eighteenth Century Goes to the Dogs. *The Colonial Williamsburg Journal* Autumn. <http://www.history.org/foundation/journal/autumn04/dogs.cfm>. Accessed 21 September 2019.

Hall, Jonathan
2017 Dogs. The Encyclopedia of Greater Philadelphia. Rutgers University, New Brunswick, NJ <https://philadelphiaencyclopedia.org/archive/dogs/>. Accessed 21 September 2019.

Howard-Smith, Stephanie
2018 Mad Dogs, Sad Dogs and the 'War against Curs' in London in 1760. *Journal for Eighteenth-Century Studies* 22(1):101–118.

Meacham, Sarah Hand
2011 Pets, Status, and Slavery in the Late-Eighteenth-Century Chesapeake. *The Journal of Southern History* 77(3):521–554.

Murden, Sarah
2019 Taxing of Dogs in the Eighteenth-Century. *Animals of the Georgian Era.*<https://georgianera.wordpress.com/2019/02/21/taxing-of-dogs-in-the-eighteenth-century/ >. Accessed 21 September 2019.

Stewart Thomson, Keith
1996 Marginalia: The Fall and Rise of the English Bulldog. *American Scientist* 84(3):220–223.

Tague, Irene
2008 Eighteenth-Century English Debates on a Dog Tax. *The Historical Journal* 51(4): 901–920.

Wagner, Katherine R.
2014 *An Osteological Analysis of 18th Century Dog Burials at the Williamsburg Public Amoury.* Undergraduate Honors Theses, Dissertations, & Master Projects. College of William and Mary, Williamsburg, VA.

Wang, Jessica
2012 Dogs and the Making of the American State: Voluntary Association, State Power, and the Politics of Animal Control in New York City, 1850-1920. *The Journal of American History* 98(4):998–1024.

A Dutch Pot from the Cradle of Religious Liberty

Richard G. Schaefer

Richard G. Schaefer

The Bowne House in Flushing, Queens, New York, is considered the oldest house in Queens County. It was first owned by Englishman John Bowne, who settled in the town of Flushing in 1654 (Figure 1) and married Hannah Feake in 1656. Tradition holds that the couple moved into the newly built Bowne House in 1661 (Brodhead 1853:705n; Wheeler 2007:2.1,2.7–2.8) (Figure 2).

A number of archaeological field schools have been conducted at the site beginning in 1984 under the direction of the late Dr. Lynn Ceci, with subsequent investigations directed by Dr. James Moore, both from Queens College CUNY (Ceci 1985; Moore 2000). Additional research was directed by the author in 2012 in expectation of planned restoration and the construction of a visitors' center (Historical Perspectives, Inc. 2012).

The pot, really a collection of sherds, was recovered during Moore's January 2001 excavation beneath the floorboards of the house's ca. 1800 eastern or "kitchen wing" (Figure 3). The scatter of artifacts may represent a sheet midden of trash tossed from a doorway in the old eastern wall of the original ca. 1661 house (Wheeler 2007:2.30; James Moore 2019, elec. comm.) (Figure 2).

Mislabeled as an "English North Devon gravel-tempered stew pot," it is actually a Dutch cooking-pot form known as a "*kookpot*" (pronounced COKE-pot, literally "cooking pot").[1] *Kookpotten* were very adaptable vessels, also serving as mixing and batter bowls, drip catchers, coin boxes, charcoal braziers, berry containers, and even musical instruments (Schaefer 1998:27,99; Janowitz and Schaefer [2020]). Seventeenth-century *kookpotten* tend to be found wherever the Dutch settled or had trading contacts. In northeastern North America, they have been recovered on Manhattan (Janowitz and Schaefer [2020]), eastern Long Island, and in the Hudson Valley (Huey 1988)—all in New Netherland—but also in Maryland (Jefferson Patterson Park and Museum 2003–2010), Newfoundland, and Quebec City.[2]

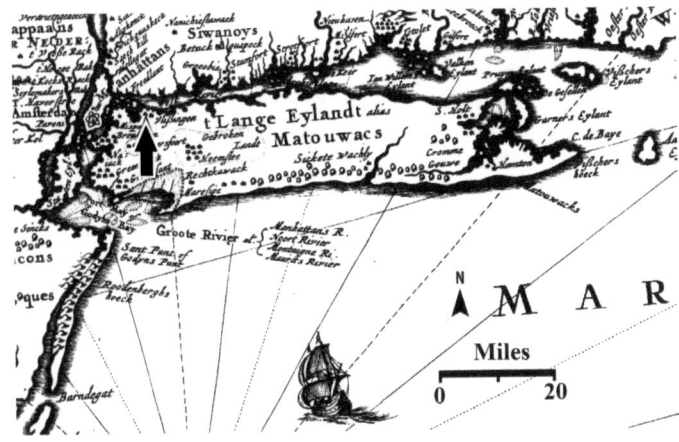

FIGURE 1. Detail of the ca. 1655 map of New Netherland and New England, showing Long Island (t Lange Eylandt), Manhattan (Manhattans) with the New Amsterdam fort, and the settlement at Flushing (Vlissingen), the latter indicated by an arrow (Visscher [1655]).

The typical 17th-century *kookpot* (Figure 4) has a globular body; a flaring, "everted bead" rim (Hurst et al. 1986:133); one or two vertical ear handles; and three stubby legs. *Kookpotten* typically have rilling on their shoulders (Figure 4*a*), but this decoration is sometimes omitted altogether (Figure 4*b–d*) or replaced with a combed band of lines (Schaefer 1998:24), as on the Bowne example (Figure 3*b*). *Kookpotten* range in height from 10 to 24 cm. Rim diameters typically vary from 10 to 24 cm, with some vessels as large as 40 cm in diameter. Their widespread use reflects the importance of soups, stews, and porridges in the 17th-century Dutch diet. The smallest *kookpotten* each have a single ear handle, perhaps with a pouring lip opposite (Figure 4*b, d*). They fulfilled the cooking, serving, and dining tasks of English pipkins, although the ear handles are distinctly Dutch (Figures 3*a*, 4, 5). The larger *kookpotten* generally had two ear handles and were mainly cooking and serving vessels, although some contemporary paintings also record their use for food consumption (Figure 5*c*) (Schaefer 1998:20–23).

Although *kookpotten* were more commonly manufactured in lead-glazed red earthenware (Figure 5a–c), the Bowne House *kookpot* is of slightly higher quality, having a buff- or white-earthenware body, with lead glaze giving it its yellow color. Sometimes copper oxide was added to the glaze, turning the vessel green, and a combination of yellow on the interior and green on the exterior was popular (Gawronski 2012:Nos. 690–695) (Figure 5d). Both the rounded bottom and feet, which made direct contact with fire, were usually left unglazed. Although the Bowne House example is incomplete, the sturdiness of the ear handle suggests that it was one of a pair (Figure 3a), and the lack of soot or burn marks on the sherds indicates that it was used for serving rather than cooking (Figure 3b).

The Bowne House and its *kookpot* survived 20th-century development because Hannah and John Bowne became Quakers. Many early Quakers were quite radical, causing public disturbances and flouting established rules of behavior (Waller 1899:46–47). On arriving in New Netherland in 1657, Quakers missionaries violated all protocols for dealing with Director-General Peter Stuyvesant and caused an uproar by going out into the streets of New Amsterdam and declaring that the "end" was near (Jacobs 2005:305–306).

Stuyvesant was unable to allay the threat of anarchy by banishing the radicals, so he imposed severe sanctions, even on people who only sheltered Quakers. In 1657, 28 residents of Flushing signed what became known as the Flushing Remonstrance, which rejected the anti-Quaker ordinances (Brodhead 1853:636–637; Waller 1899:39–43). Although popularly hailed as a landmark in the struggle for freedom of conscience (Moyer 2004), it was not. Freedom of conscience was already guaranteed in New Netherland. What *was* illegal was disturbing the peace and the holding of public services by non-Calvinist groups—including other Protestants. The Remonstrance is better described as a milestone in the separation of church and state (Driscoll 2005; Jacobs 2005:305–308).

Hannah Bowne converted to Quakerism and became a preacher, and John converted shortly after (Brodhead 1853:705; Reynolds 1911:228–232). In 1662, John was arrested for hosting services in his house. He disrespected authority by not removing his hat before Stuyvesant and refusing to pay the imposed fine. Imprisoned and banished to Amsterdam to be judged by Stuyvesant's superiors, the Dutch West India Company directors, he was eventually freed, and Stuyvesant was instructed to ignore the Quakers as long as they caused no trouble (Waller 1899:43–45; Jacobs 2005:310–311).

Quaker-written histories embellished the incident and hailed Bowne's "triumphant" return and Stuyvesant's "well-earned rebuke" (Yarnall 1908:45–53), turning the house into a pilgrimage stop for touring Quakers to this day. Bowne descendants were conscious of John and Hannah's role in these events, and the house, although enlarged and altered, was protected and occupied by Bowne descendants well into the 20th century (Yarnall 1908:44; Haywood 1931), thus escaping the wrecker's ball.

FIGURE 2. The Bowne House, 1825, view toward the northeast (Milbert 1825). The original ca. 1661 section of the house is outlined in white. The one-story, ca. 1800 kitchen wing, beneath which the *kookpot* was found, is immediately adjacent to the east (*right*).

Richard G. Schaefer

FIGURE 3. The Bowne House *kookpot* sherds, white earthenware, lead glaze, post-1660: (a) Ear handle (shown upside down, with rim end on the bottom); (b) body sherd showing glazed shoulder with combed or incised rilling, and an unglazed and unburnt bottom; and (c) part of the rim, too fragmentary to determine diameter (Photograph by Sara F. Mascia, 2012).

A Dutch Pot from the Cradle of Religious Liberty

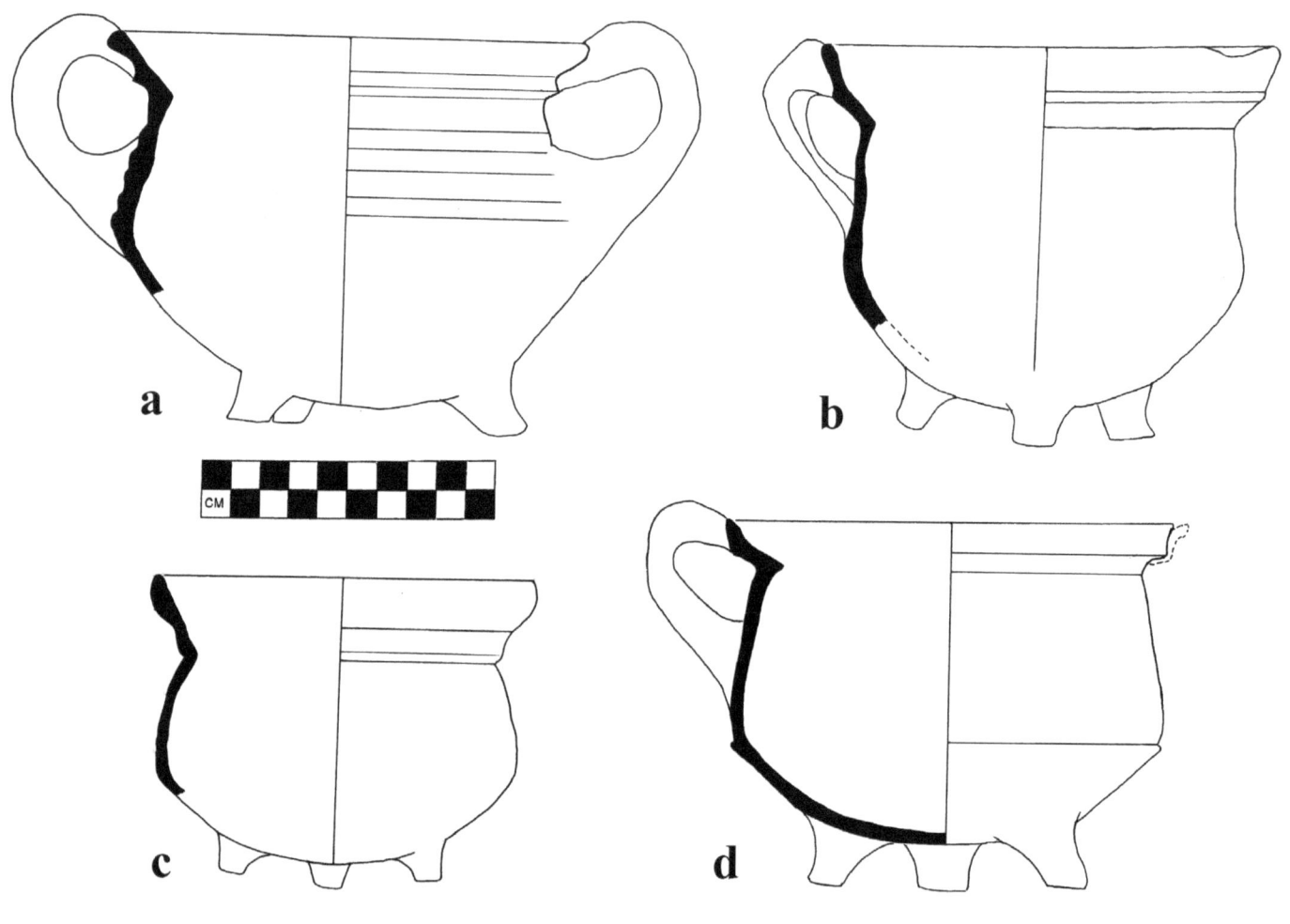

FIGURE 4. Lead-glazed, red-earthenware, 17th-century *kookpotten* excavated in the Netherlands: (*a*) *Kookpot* with two ear handles, burnt, from Bergen op Zoom, 1600–1625 (Schaefer 1998:fig. 10.3); (*b*) *kookpot* with a single ear handle and pouring lip, white slip on the interior, glazed to the feet, from Bergen op Zoom, 1650–1700 (Schaefer 1998: fig. 13.3); (*c*) *kookpot* with a single ear handle (not shown), all surfaces glazed, from Bergen op Zoom, 1650–1700 (Schaefer 1998:fig. 10.2); and (*d*) *kookpot* with a single ear handle and pouring lip, bottom and feet unglazed, from Amsterdam (Schaefer 1998:fig. 12.1).

Richard G. Schaefer

FIGURE 5. *Kookpotten* from 17th-century Dutch paintings: (*a*) A red-earthenware *kookpot* overturned on the floor, Jan Steen, *The Pastry Seller* (detail), ca. 1660, Musée des Beaux-Arts de Rouen; (*b*) a small pipkin-sized, red-earthenware *kookpot* with a spoon used to feed a child, Gabriel Metsu, *The Sick Child* (detail), ca. 1660, Rijksmuseum Trippenhuis, Amsterdam; (*c*) a very large two-eared, red-earthenware *kookpot*, Gerard Dou, *Woman Eating Porridge* (detail), 1632–1637, Sotheby's New York; and (*d*) a two-eared, white-earthenware *kookpot*, glazed green on the exterior and yellow on the interior, used to mix and spoon out pancake batter, Gabriel Metsu, *The Pancake Maker* (detail), 1665–1668, Gemäldegalerie, Berlin (Figure by author, 2019; painting images from <https://commons.wikimedia.org>).

How did a late 17th-century Dutch vessel end up in a trash heap adjacent to an English house in an English town? It was possibly brought by canoe from New Amsterdam on Manhattan Island to Flushing, where the Bownes could have purchased it (W. W. Munsell & Co. 1882:77). A more interesting possibility is that John Bowne acquired the pot during his so-called banishment. He was put ashore in Ireland and, unaccompanied, made a leisurely trip through England, where he visited and socialized with Quaker compatriots, even meeting founder George Fox along the way (Yarnall 1908:50–51). While in Amsterdam in 1663, Bowne daily encountered the vast array of consumer goods for which the city was known. He was likely familiar with the outdoor Noordermarkt (Northern Market)—specializing in old housewares, clothing, and ceramics—located near Dutch West India Company headquarters, where his case was being heard (Gellinek 1988:369). Bowne did not resist the urge to shop: in a letter to Hannah in June 1663, he wrote that "I have sent thee a trunk full of things" (Yarnall 1908:51).

A third possibility is that Hannah Bowne purchased the *kookpot* herself. In the 1670s, she undertook two Quaker missionary trips to England, Holland, and Friesland on her own, the latter places being Dutch centers of white-earthenware production. Unfortunately, the second trip ended in London, where she died in 1677 (Yarnall 1908:58–62).

The Bowne House and its Dutch *kookpot*, both remarkable survivors, provide a direct and tangible link to a turbulent time. It is hoped that greater awareness of this vessel form will lead to the identification of *kookpotten* in more archaeological collections, so that their stories may also be told.

Acknowledgments

Thank you to Dr. James Moore and Queens College CUNY for opening their Bowne House collection to me, generously sharing data, and granting me permission to publish on this fascinating artifact.

A Dutch Pot from the Cradle of Religious Liberty

RICHARD G. SCHAEFER

Historical Perspectives, Inc.
PO Box 529
Westport, CT 06881, USA

References

Brodhead, John Romeyn
1853 *History of the State of New York*, Vol.1. Harper and Brothers, New York, NY.

Ceci, Lynn
1985 Historical Archaeology at the 1661 John Browne House, Flushing, New York. Report to Bowne House Historical Society, Flushing, NY, from Department of Anthropology, Queens College CUNY, Flushing, NY.

Driscoll, James
2005 *Flushing 1880–1935*. Arcadia, Charleston, SC.

Gawronski, Jerzy (editor)
2012 *Amsterdam Ceramics: A City's History and an Archaeological Ceramics Catalogue 1175–2011*. Uitgeverij Bas Lubberhuizen/Bureau Monumenten & Archeologie, Amsterdam, the Netherlands.

Gellinek, Christian (editor)
1988 *Europas Erster Baedeker: Filip von Zesens Amsterdam 1664 (Europe's first Baedeker: Filip von Zesen's Amsterdam 1664)*. Peter Lang, New York, NY.

Haywood, Dorothy
1931 Flushing Birthplace of Freedom Remains Untouched by Machine Age as Owners Preserve Charm of Colonial Days. *Brooklyn Daily Star* 26 September:1.

Historical Perspectives, Inc.
2012 Archaeological Documentary Study: Bowne House, 37-01 Bowne Street, Flushing, Queens, New York 10014, Block 5013 Lot 6. Report to New York City Department of Parks, New York, NY, from Historical Perspectives, Inc., Westport, CT.

Huey, Paul R.
1988 Aspects of Continuity and Change in Colonial Dutch Material Culture at Fort Orange, 1624–1664. Doctoral dissertation, Department of American Civilization, University of Pennsylvania, Philadelphia. University Microfilms International, Ann Arbor, MI.

Hurst, John G., David S. Neal, and H. J. E. van Beuningen
1986 *Pottery Produced and Traded in North-West Europe 1350–1650*. Museum Boymans van Beuningen, Stichting "Het Nederlands Gerbruiksvoorwerp," Rotterdam Papers VI. Rotterdam, the Netherlands.

Jacobs, Jaap
2005 *New Netherland: A Dutch Colony in Seventeenth-Century America*. Brill, Leiden, the Netherlands.

Janowitz, Meta F., and Richard G. Schaefer
[2020] By any other Name: Kookpotten or Grapen? Little Pots, Big Stories. In *The Archaeology of New Netherland: Uncovering a Forgotten World*, Craig Lukezic and John P. McCarthy, editors. University Press of Florida, Gainesville.

Jefferson Patterson Park and Museum
2003–2010 18CV279, Vessel #24, Top, Dutch Pipkin. Compton 18CV279, Archaeological Collections in Maryland, Jefferson Patterson Park and Museum <https://apps.jefpat.maryland.gov/NEH/DetailImages.aspx?ImageNo=cv279-00059s>. Accessed 18 September 2019.

Milbert, Jacques Gérard
1825 *View of Flushing (Long Island), North America: Mr. Bowne's House It Remains in the Possession of His Family ever since 1661 Time when It Was Built*. Charles Etienne Motte [lithographer], Paris, France.

Moore, James A.
2000 Bowne House Stabilization Project: Archaeological Assessment Proposal, 29 April. Manuscript, Department of Anthropology, Queens College, Flushing, NY.

Moyer, Theresa
2004 "To Have and Enjoy the Liberty of Conscience": Community-Responsive Museum Education at the Bowne House. *In Places in the Mind: Public Archaeology as Applied Anthropology*, Paul Shackel and Erve Chambers, editors, pp. 85–100. Routledge, New York, NY.

Reynolds, Cuyler (editor)
  1911 *Hudson—Mohawk Genealogical and Family Memoirs*, Vol. 1. Lewis Historical, New York, NY.

Schaefer, Richard G.
  1998 *A Typology of Seventeenth-Century Dutch Ceramics and Its Implications for American Historical Archaeology*. British Archaeological Reports, International Series 702. John and Erica Hedges, Oxford, UK.

Visscher, Claes Janszoon
  [1655] *Novi Belgii Novaeque Angliae: nec non partis Virginiae* (New Netherland New England: As well as part of Virginia). Claes Janszoon Visscher, Amsterdam, the Netherlands.

Waller, Henry D.
  1899 *History of the Town of Flushing, Long Island, New York*. J. H. Ridenour, Flushing, NY. Reprinted 1975 by Harbor Hill, Harrison, NY.

Wheeler, Walter Richard
  2007 The Bowne House: Flushing, Queens County, New York: An Historic Structure Report. Report to Bowne House Historical Society, Flushing, NY, from Hartgen Archaeological Associates, Inc., Rensselaer, NY.

W. W. Munsell & Co.
  1882 *History of Queens County*, New York. W. W. Munsell & Co., New York, NY.

Yarnall, Charles
  1908 John Bowne of Flushing. *Bulletin of Friends' Historical Society of Philadelphia* 2(2):44–67.

Endnotes

[1] Until fairly recently, Dutch archaeologists have called this vessel a *"grape"* (CHRAH-peh). Although this term has been superseded by the more-correct *"kookpot,"* *"grape"* is not uncommon in Dutch archaeological literature and many museum catalogs (Janowitz and Schaefer [2020]).

[2] The Quebec *kookpot* was part of an archaeological display in the lobby of the Auberge Saint-Antoine, where it was misidentified as "English."

Form or Function? Attempting to Identify a Reason for Decorating Kiln Stilts

Linda Stone

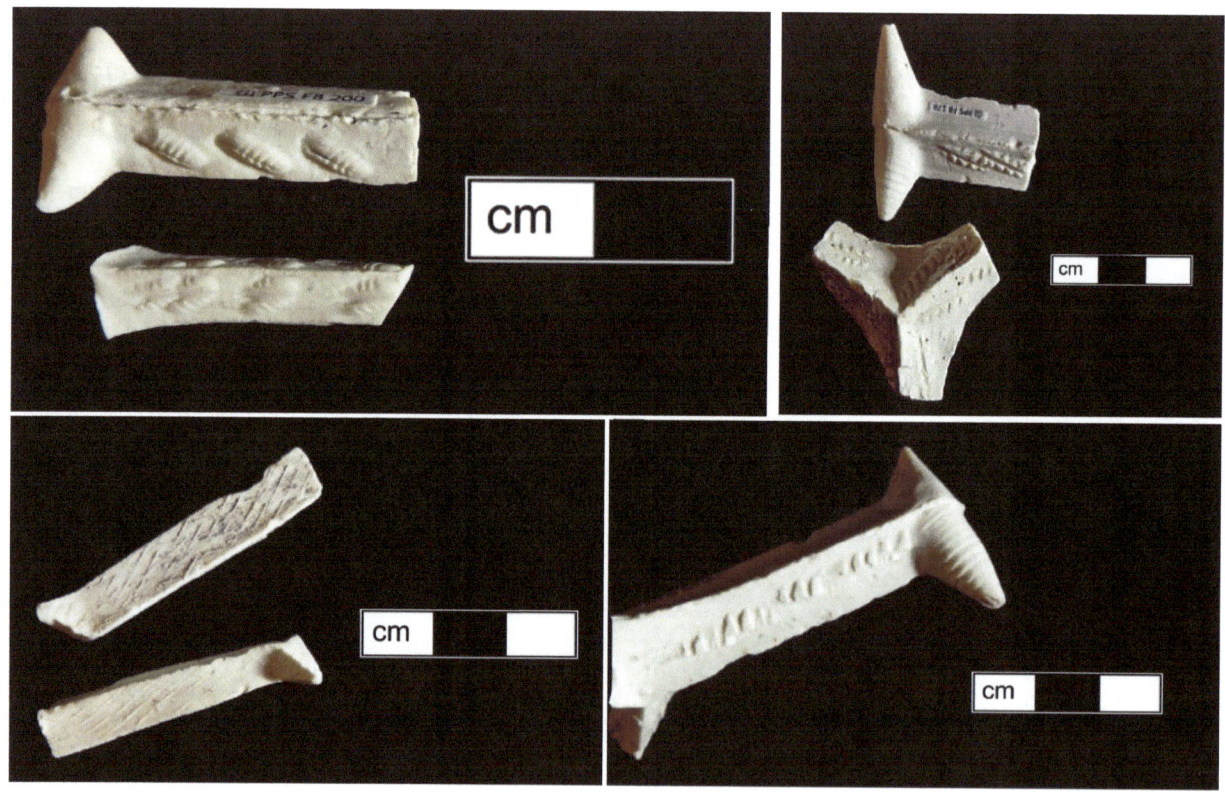

Mysterious kiln stilts have been found in fill on Governors Island in New York Harbor. The mystery has to do with both how the stilts got to Governors Island and why they were embossed with repetitive decoration, if one could call it decoration.

A sizable amount of kiln waste from an unknown source has been identified in historic fill unearthed on Governors Island, New York. There is no history of ceramic production there. The kiln waste is representative of a variety of ware types and several forms of kiln furniture, but primarily stilts. The embossed stilts include examples with maker's marks, numbers, letters, or motifs. However, on a given stilt, there is typically only one of these elements.

Governors Island is now a 172-acre park in the middle of New York Harbor off the tip of lower Manhattan in New York City (Figure 1). Prior to European settlement, Governors Island was used intermittently by Native Americans. Once the Dutch arrived, recognizing the strategic position of the Island within the harbor, they quickly set up shop there, building a small fort. Throughout much of its history, Governors Island remained a military outpost. British and then American armies occupied the island. After the American army relocated in 1966, the U.S. Coast Guard moved in. They stayed until 1996 when the island was deeded to New York by then President Bill Clinton. Much rehabilitation to Governors Island has taken place since and continues to date.

Although all this background information is relevant, the most important thing about Governors Island is that it is shaped like an ice cream cone. The ice cream portion was the original landform and now contains Governors Island National Monument and Governors Island Historic District, which includes two forts and other historic structures and features. The cone portion of the island was added beginning in 1911, more than doubling the island's size, with the addition of fill from the excavation of the Lexington Avenue subway. This part of Governors Island has recently been transformed into parkland for public enjoyment.

The legend of the Lexington Avenue subway fill on Governors Island overshadows a smaller, lesser-known fill episode that happened about thirty years earlier. In 1883, a seawall perimeter was constructed around the entire then extant island (the ice cream). It is the fill added during this project in which the kiln waste was found, not in the well-known, and later, Lexington Avenue subway fill.

The 1867 map of Governors Island "from a survey made under the direction of General John G. Barnard" provides a snapshot of the shoreline at that time, showing primarily a beach with shoreline retention structures present only in limited places (Figure 2). A second map dating to 1906 was drawn by J.M. Hilton after the new seawall had been constructed. Figure 3 is a copy of that map overlaid with the footprint of the original landform thereby showing just how much land was added.

The majority of the kiln waste has thus far been documented in fill primarily located near South Battery, where the largest exposure of that deposit was disturbed as a result of landscaping and work on utility upgrades. Plans for that project triggered archaeological excavation dictated by historic preservation and environmental review laws. Although this is the largest area of kiln waste fill documented on Governors Island to date, the kiln waste deposit has also been identified near the former shoreline in other places on the island.

Recovered kiln stilts were often marked or decorated, but many more undecorated pieces were also present. The only maker's mark represented in the deposit is B & Co, which was found on a number of the stilts (Figure 4). This mark is attributed to W.W. Buller and Company of Hanley in Staffordshire, England. They were in business under that name from 1862 to 1883 (Allied Insulators Ltd. 2011). Other artifacts found in association with the fill narrow the date of deposition to no earlier than the early 1880s (Stone 2016:66–67). In addition to the maker's mark, other stilts are marked with numbers, or letters, or both (Figure 5). These marks may represent stilt sizes (Dransfield 2009:14).

Examples of the decorated kiln stilts are shown in Figure 6. Research conducted as part of several archaeological projects and subsequent presentations on the subject has resulted in no information on these designs. Therefore, the author has

Form or Function? Attempting to Identify a Reason for Decorating Kiln Stilts

47

FIGURE 1. *Left* Map of New York City with Governors Island highlighted (<https://commons.wikimedia.org> marked by author); *right* Governors Island park map (Courtesy of the Trust for Governors Island).

ascribed pattern names to the embossed motifs: snail shell, triangles, leaf (perhaps multiple triangles), and cross hatch. The patterns, when present, occur on two faces of the stilt arms. Among the Governors Island samples, the only pattern that is also sometimes marked is the cross hatch.

After consulting with numerous ceramic specialists in the United States, including those represented in this volume, it appears Governors Island is the only archaeological site in the country where marked or decorated kiln stilts have been found.

Only one ceramic researcher has thus far been identified who had seen these types of stilts in archaeological context, or any other context for that matter. David Barker, a ceramic specialist in Staffordshire who has conducted research on W.

W. Buller & Company, has seen these types of decorated stilts. However, he does not know if they were produced by that company. When asked about the decorations and whether he knew of any pattern names for them, his answer was surprising. He had not previously thought of these embossings as decorations, but rather as utilitarian texturizing designed to prevent the potters' fingers from burning (David Barker 2015, elec. comm.).

Identifying a researcher in England who has seen these objects leads one to conclude that England was the original source of the kiln stilts. This conclusion implies one of three scenarios: either the stilts were purchased from a British supplier for use in a kiln(s) in the United States; they were inadvertently included in shipments of ceramics from

48

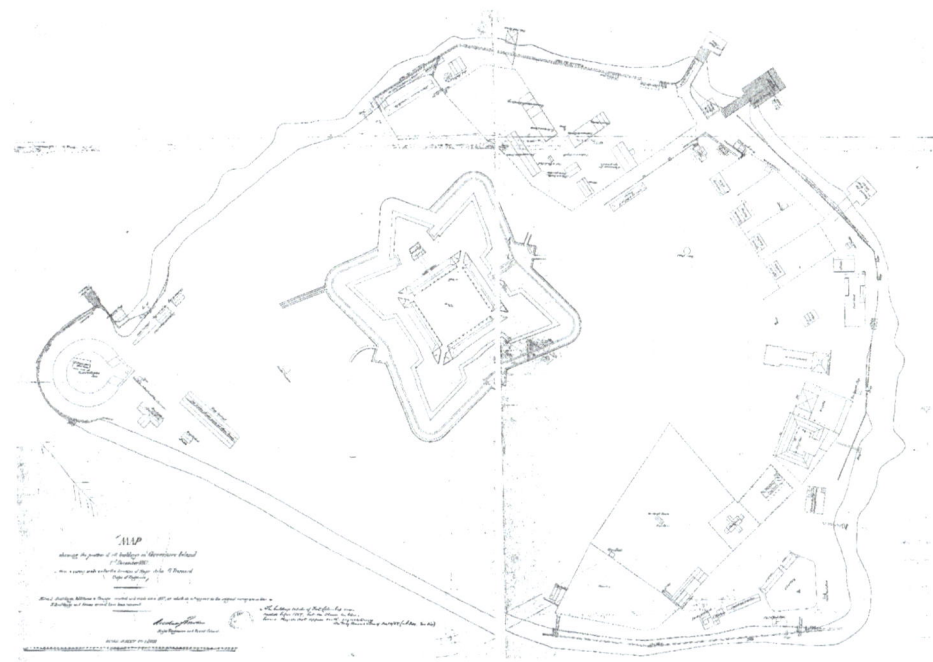

FIGURE 2. 1867 Map of Governors Island. U.S. Army Corps of Engineers. Surveyed by Major John G. Barnard (National Archives Fortification File, Drawer 37, Sheet 55).

FIGURE 3. 1906 Governors Island, New York overlaid with the footprint of the shoreline prior to landfilling. Map drawn by J.M. Hilton, "photographed Oct.10, 1903, corrected Apr. 16, 1906, Apr. 24, 06, May 23, 06, Jun. 21, 06." (National Archives, College Park Maryland. RG 92; Blueprint File; Governors Island, NY).

Form or Function? Attempting to Identify a Reason for Decorating Kiln Stilts

FIGURE 4. Governors Island kiln stilt marked: B & Co (Photograph by author, 2018).

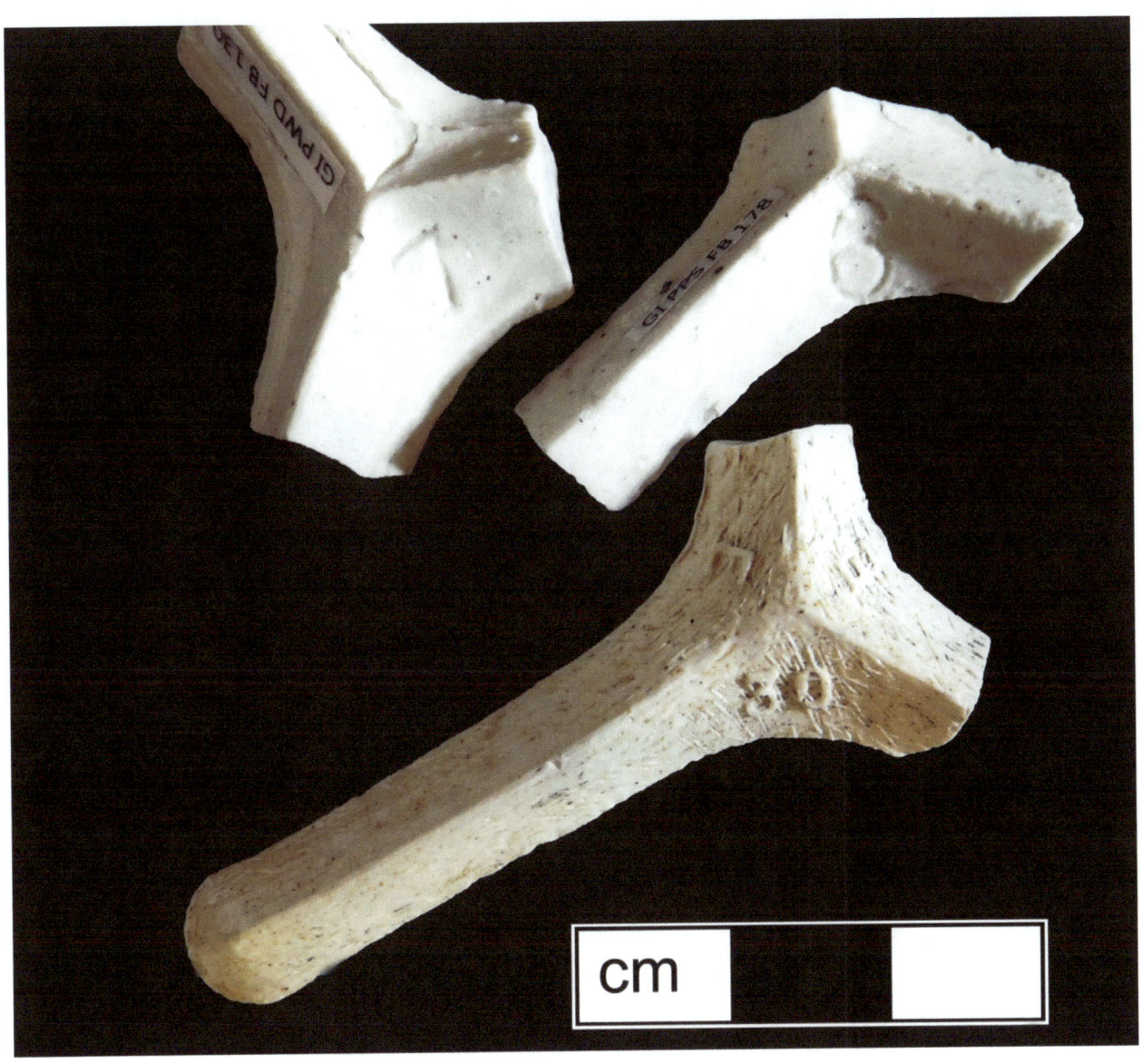

FIGURE 5. Governors Island kiln stilts embossed with numbers and letters: *top to bottom*, 7, 6, E, and 30 (Photograph by author, 2018).

Form or Function? Attempting to Identify a Reason for Decorating Kiln Stilts

51

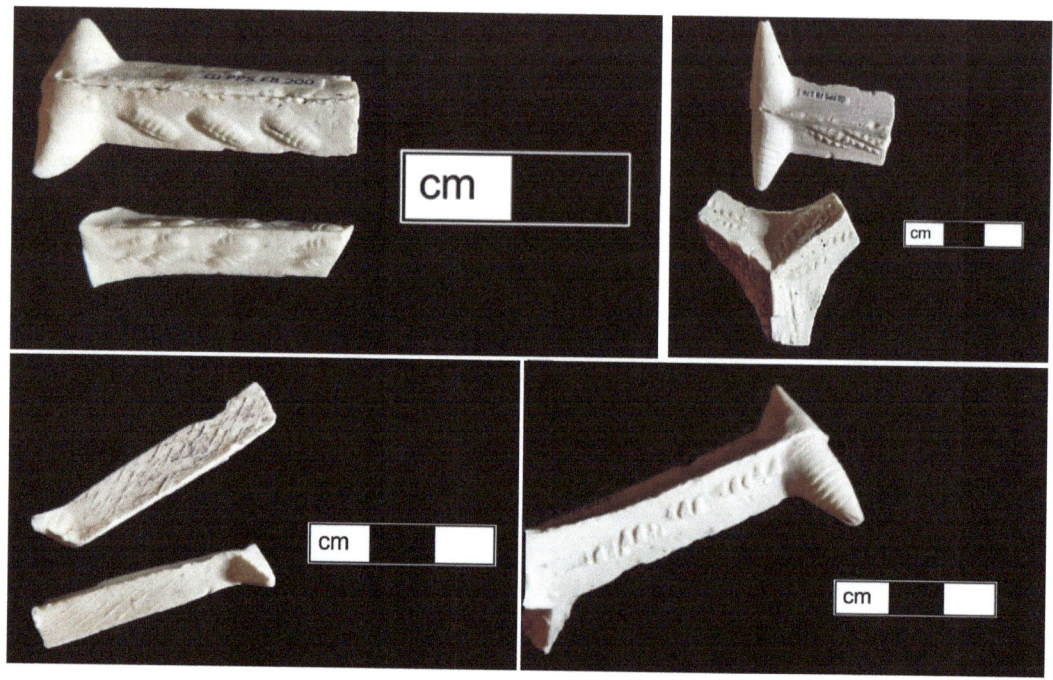

FIGURE 6. Governors Island kiln stilts with repetitive embossed motifs; *clockwise from upper left,* shell, leaf, triangle, and cross hatch (Photograph by author, 2018).

Staffordshire; or the fill containing the stilts originated in England. A potential importer of these types of kiln stilts in the New York City region has not yet been identified, but this seems the most likely scenario. The possibility that the stilts were inadvertently contained in a shipment of ceramics seems unlikely because of the presence of wasters, some only bisque fired, in the deposit. The presence of imported fill, however unlikely it seems, may not be totally out of the question. The importation of fill as ballast has been documented at archaeological sites throughout the northeastern United States (LeeDecker et al. 1994:table 6.1). However, all of these sites date from prior to 1883 when Governors Island was filled and none of those sites have documented fill coming from across the Atlantic.

So, whether it be form or function, the mystery remains as to why the stilts were embossed and how they got to Governors Island in New York. Any information on these stilts you may have or come across would be much appreciated by the author.

Acknowledgements

Thank you to the Trust for Governors Island for the opportunity to work in such a magnificent setting, to Jenna Wallace Coplin for her research in identifying the maker of the marked stilts, and to Meta Janowitz for her research suggestions and for showing the stilts around at "dish camp."

Linda Stone

LINDA STONE

Archaeological Consultant in New York City
249 E. 48 St., #12B
New York, NY 10017, USA

References

Allied Insulators Limited
    2011 Company History web page <http://www.alliedinsulators.com/company/history/>. Page copyright 2011. Accessed 9 September 2014.

Dransfield, Neil
    2009 Strongford Mill, Stoke on Trent, Staffordshire, Archaeological Assessment and Final Report, ARCUS report 1097b.1(1) © AROUS 2008. Report to Severn Trent Water, from University of Sheffield, Sheffield, UK. February 2009.

LeeDecker, Charles H., Edward M. Morin, Ingrid Wuebber, Meta Janowitz, Marie-Lorraine Pipes, Nadia Shevchuk, Mallory Gordon, and Diane Dallal
    1994 The Meadows Site (36PH35), Archaeological Data Recovery Program, I-95 Completion Project, Philadelphia, Philadelphia County, Pennsylvania, ER# 82-0230-101-V. Report to Pennsylvania Department of Transportation Engineering District 6-0 and the Federal Highway Administration and Urban Engineers, Inc., Philadelphia, PA, from the Cultural Resource Group, Louis Berger & Associates Inc., East Orange, NJ. February 1994.

Stone, Linda
    2016 Report on the Governors Island Potable Water Source & Distribution Project - Phase II of Governors Island, New York, New York. OPRHP Project Review No. 13PR03803. Report to the Trust for Governors Island, New York, NY, from Linda Stone, MA, RPA, New York, NY. March 31, 2016.

Diamonds and Triangles: Two Locally-Made Pipes from the 17th-century Chesapeake

Lauren McMillan

Two 17th-century tobacco pipe fragments have been identified from two sites in Westmoreland County, Virginia that appear to combine decorative traditions from two, perhaps three, different groups living in the area at the time: Native Virginians, English colonists, and possibly enslaved Africans. Both pipes, one recovered from a mid-17th-century domestic refuse midden at Nomini Plantation (44WM12) and one unprovenienced from the John Washington Site (44WM204), have nearly identical decorative patterns and similar manufacturing techniques (Figures 1 and 2). These two sites are located approximately 10 miles apart on the southern banks of the Potomac River and were connected through political and familial networks in the middle of the 17th century (Hatch 2015:98–106).

Both of these pipe stems, made of local Chesapeake clay, are light reddish brown and have bore diameters of 11/64 in. Both stems have a series of banded decorations consisting of rouletted lines, diamonds with stylized dots in the center, and triangles—combining English pipe decorative motifs of the "Bristol diamond" pattern (Hurry and Keeler 1991; figure 1) and "hanging triangles" (Mouer et al. 1999:103; figure 3) from Native Algonquian-style pottery and pipes. Diamonds were used by Native peoples in the Chesapeake and by Africans, in addition to Europeans. The presence of a central stamp creating a dot indicates that these diamonds were meant to imitate the Bristol-made pipes of the same time period. There are slight differences between the two pipes. The example from Nomini Plantation has clear smoothing lines, as opposed to the John Washington Site example, which was not smoothed as heavily. The stem from Nomini Plantation shows evidence of heavy use of white infill, whereas as the Washington site stem has very little evidence of white infill.

While the overall "grammar" of the two pipes is consistent, with the bands, diamonds, and triangles appearing in the same order, how they were executed differs. Two different rouletting and stamping tool sets were used to produce the decorations. The Nomini Plantation example is more crisp and clean with clear delineations between each motif compared to the Washington Site stem. There are slight variations in the number of lines within each horizontal band, the elongation of the diamonds, and the height of the triangles. Based on archaeological and historical evidence, the Nomini Plantation example was most likely produced on the site; indirect evidence suggests that the Washington Site example may have been made at the same location. Questions of who produced these pipes and who had influence over the design attributes can possibly be answered by looking to the historical record.

Nomini Plantation was home to various people, named and unnamed, throughout its occupation from 1647 until 1722 (McMillan 2015:197–200). Members of the Speke family appear in the historical records most frequently (Hatch and McMillan 2019). Thomas Speke founded the plantation in 1647. His second wife, Frances Gerrard, remained on the property until her death ca. 1691 (Sherman and Mitchell 1983:107). Frances married John Washington (at whose site one of the pipes in question was found) in 1676 but remained at Nomini Plantation during their short-lived marriage prior to his death in 1677 (Toner 1891:202).

Beyond the Speke/Gerrard family, Thomas Speke's 1659 will and 1660 probate inventory indicates there were 11 servants, including 3 Africans living on the property (LOV 1653–1671:103–105, 1661–1662:4a–6a). The fact that the servants listed as "negroe" did not have their remaining time to serve recorded, like the other eight, suggests that Tom, Mary, and Frances were in lifelong enslavement and were not indentured servants. Coombs (2011) has argued that

FIGURE 1 (opposite page). Tobacco pipe stems from Nomini Plantation (44WM12). Top: English white ball clay tobacco pipes with "Bristol diamond" motif. Bottom: Local handmade pipe with diamond and triangle decoration (Photograph by author, 2013). Courtesy of the Virginia Department of Historic Resources.

FIGURE 2. Local handmade pipe stem with diamond and triangle decoration from the John Washington Site (44WM204) (Photograph by D. Brad Hatch, 2013). Courtesy of Colonial Encounters and the National Park Service, George Washington Birthplace National Monument, GEWA 4849.

only members of the gentry class owned enslaved Africans and African Americans prior to the 1670s and that slavery did not become prominent on the Northern Neck until after the 1730s, making Nomini Plantation an interesting location to investigate early evidence of intercultural interaction via material culture.

In a 1659 deed of land transfer, William Hardidge I, who owned the land adjoining Nomini Plantation to the west, described his property boundary as "...near the side of an Indian field commonly known as the Pipemaker's field" (LOV 1653–1671:11–12). Further evidence to support the assertion

that the pipe maker lived on Speke's property includes the presence of handmade pipe wasters in the bottom two layers of the refuse midden; these two layers date to the last half of the 17th century. This deed reference and the form of the pipes recovered (that of Algonquian-speaking Indians), suggests that the majority of the pipes made at Nomini Plantation were likely the products of the Indian pipe maker(s) and were made in the third quarter of the 17th century. However, a known Native Virginian making pipes on the site does not eliminate the possibility of other influences on the decorations.

Lauren McMillan

FIGURE 3. Potomac Creek Pottery from the Potomac Creek Site (44ST2) (Photograph by the author, 2019). Courtesy of the Smithsonian Institution, Museum of Natural History, Department of Anthropology.

FIGURE 4. Deer pipe from Nomini Plantation (44WM12) (Photograph by the author, 2014). Courtesy of the Virginia Department of Historic Resources.

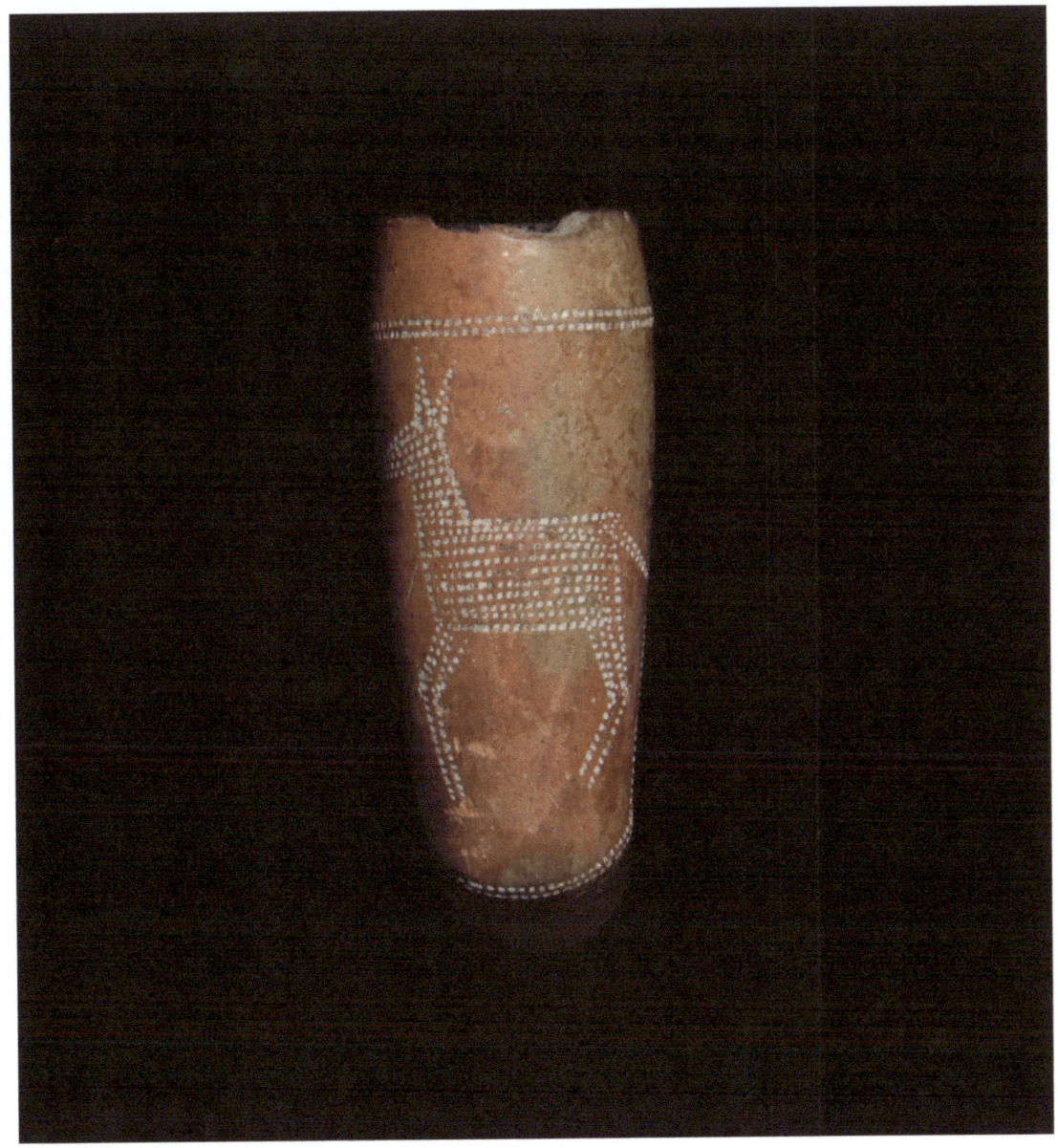

FIGURE 5. Deer pipe from the Chesopean site (44VB48) (Photograph by Katherine Ridgway, 2019).
Courtesy of the Virginia Department of Historic Resources.

One of the more interesting questions about these two handmade pipes is why the pipe maker(s) chose to combine these two motifs: English Bristol diamonds and Algonquian hanging triangles, especially since many of the colonial pipe makers in the area who were producing mold-made pipes were copying Dutch decorative motifs (McMillan 2015:250–276). Perhaps the Bristol diamond decoration is related to John Washington and his marriage to Frances; John was a merchant with strong connections to the Bristol trade (Hatch 1979).

The use of the hanging triangle decoration is clearly derived from Algonquian pottery predating European contact (Mouer et al. 1999:103) and perhaps illustrates some influences from West African stylistic traditions (Emerson 1988, 1999). The triangles could represent a shared cultural motif between two or three of the groups present on the site — Native Virginians, enslaved Africans, and European colonists. These combined motifs are illustrative of the creolization processes that were occurring on the site and in the Chesapeake in the middle of the 17th century (Mouer et al. 1999:116). The interactions and exchanges of ideas and decorative patterns that occurred at Nomini Plantation may also account for why the designs produced on the site, particularly the running deer motif, were often more geometric and abstract than most other examples in the Chesapeake (Figures 4 and 5). The majority of locally-made handcrafted pipes in the 17th-century Chesapeake were most likely not manufactured by Africans and African Americans, given the low population numbers of the time (Walsh 2001; Coombs 2011), but instead by local Algonquian-speaking people who made this type of pipe long before European colonization. However, there is clear historical evidence from Nomini Plantation that African influence may have been possible.

Several different groups of people occupied and frequented Nomini Plantation throughout the 17th century: English colonial yeomen, European indentured servants, enslaved Africans, and Native Virginians. Each of these groups brought with them their own cultural ideas of what their material world should look like and how to decorate their objects, even the most mundane and ubiquitous (although, for some, pipes may not have been secular and ordinary, but sacred and extraordinary). Historical and archaeological evidence is highly suggestive that these two pipes with diamond and triangle motifs were produced at Nomini Plantation by a local Algonquian maker or makers, influenced by contemporary English design, and possibly by African design elements. These pipes represent a confluence of distinct peoples— Native Virginian, African, and English —coming together in the creation of a new society.

LAUREN MCMILLAN
University of Mary Washington
Department of Historic Preservation
1301 College Avenue
Fredericksburg, VA 22401, USA

References

Colonial Encounters Project
2013 John Washington Site (44WM204). Colonial Encounters: The Lower Potomac River Valley at Contact, 1500-1720AD < http://colonialencounters.org>. Accessed 18 November 2019.

Coombs, John. C.
2011 The Phases of Conversion: A New Chronology for the Rise of Slavery in Early Virginia. *The William and Mary Quarterly* 68(3):332–360.

Emerson, Matthew C.
1988 *Decorated Clay Tobacco Pipes from the Chesapeake*. Doctoral dissertation, Department of Anthropology, University of California, Berkeley, CA. UMI International, Ann Arbor, MI.

1999 African Inspiration in a New World Art and Artifact: Decorated Pipes from the Chesapeake. In *'I, Too, Am America:' Archaeological Studies of African-American Life*, Theresa A. Singleton, editor, pp. 47–82. University of Virginia Press, Charlottesville.

Hatch, Charles E., Jr.
1979 *Popes Creek Plantation: Birthplace of George Washington*. The Wakefield National Memorial Association, Washington's Birthplace, VA.

Hatch, D. Brad
2015 An Historical Archaeology of Early Modern Manhood in the Potomac River Valley of Virginia, 1645–1730. Doctoral dissertation, Department of Anthropology, University of Tennessee, Knoxville.

Hatch, D. Brad and Lauren K. McMillan
2019 Reanalyzing, Reinterpreting, and Rediscovering the Appamattucks Community. In *New Life for Old Collections*, Rebecca Allen and Ben Ford, editors, pp. 145–72. University of Nebraska Press, Lincoln.

Hurry, Silas D. and Robert W. Keeler
1991 A Descriptive Analysis of the White Clay Tobacco Pipes from the St. John's Site is St. Mary's City, Maryland. *In The Archaeology of the Clay Tobacco Pipe XII, Chesapeake Bay*, Peter Davey and Dennis J. Pogue, editors, pp. 37–71. British Archaeological Reports International Series 56. British Archaeological Reports, Oxford, UK.

Library of Virginia (LOV)
1653–1671 Westmoreland County Deeds and Wills, No. 1, microfilm reel 2. Library of Virginia, Richmond.
1661–1662 Westmoreland County Deeds, Wills, Etc., microfilm reel 1. Library of Virginia, Richmond.

McMillan, Lauren K.
2015 Community Formation and the Development of a British-Atlantic Identity in the Chesapeake: An Archaeological and Historical Study of the Tobacco Pipe Trade in the Potomac River Valley ca. 1630–1730. Doctoral dissertation, Department of Anthropology, University of Tennessee, Knoxville.

Mouer, Daniel L., Mary Ellen N. Hodges, Stephen R. Potter, Susan L. Henry Renaud, Ivor Noël Hume, Dennis J. Pogue, Martha W. McCartney, and Thomas E. Davidson
1999 Colonoware Pottery, Chesapeake Pipes, and "Uncritical Assumptions." In *'I, Too, Am America:' Archaeological Studies of African-American Life*, Theresa A. Singleton, editor, pp. 83-115. University of Virginia Press, Charlottesville.

Sherman, Virginia W., and Vivienne Mitchell
1983 Nominy Plantation. In *Westmoreland County, Virginia: 1653–1983*, Walter Briscoe Norris, Jr., editor, pp. 105–110. Westmoreland County Board of Supervisors, Montross, VA.

Toner, Joseph M.
1891 Wills of the American Ancestors of General George Washington. *The New England Historical and Genealogical Register* 45:199–215.

Walsh, Lorena S.
2001 The Chesapeake Slave Trade: Regional Patterns, African Origins, and Some Implications. *The William and Mary Quarterly* 58(1):139–170.

Not All Decorated Salt-Glazed Stoneware is German:

GR Medallions on Stoneware made in New York City

Meta F. Janowitz

Vessels produced by 18th-century stoneware potters working in the Northeast have been *terra incognita* (pun intended) until recently. Antiquarians interested in material culture began studying locally made ceramics at the turn of the 20th century by perusing 19th-century documents and talking to potters still operating in a craft tradition; they worked backward to reconstruct the history of American pottery production from the perspective of their own time (Barber 1893, 1903, 1904; Pitkin 1917). Later historians, such as Robert Sim and Arthur Clement (1944) and Lura Woodside Watkins (1950), excavated old pottery sites, acquiring examples of kiln wasters. Nineteenth-century vessels in museum and private collections were described and attributed to potters based on makers' marks and decorative elements.

By the time the African Burial Ground in New York City was excavated in the early 1990s (Cheek and Roberts 2009a, 2009b; Perry et al. 2009), much had been discovered about 19th-century potters in the northeastern United States. Lacking direct evidence, ceramic historians seem to have concluded that 18th-century potters made more or less the same types of vessels with the same types of decorations as were made a century later: above-ground evidence of early production in the form of waster dumps was absent or unidentified; documents relating to early potteries were rare; and few extant vessels could be attributed unequivocally to early potters because most vessels were not signed or marked by their makers until the end of the 18th century. Signed vessels were, almost exclusively, presentation pieces with elaborate decorations, for example an inkwell/inkstand made in 1773 by William Crolius (The Metropolitan Museum of Art 2000–2019a).

In general, historical archaeologists followed the lead of ceramic historians and assumed there were no significant differences between 18th- and 19th-century locally made pots. Recent archaeological projects and documentary research have revealed this is incorrect, at least for salt-glazed stonewares. One such project was the excavation of the

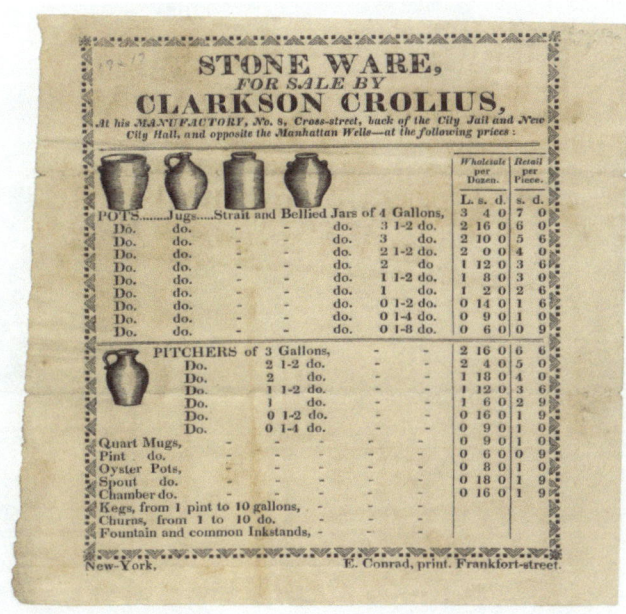

FIGURE 1. Early 19th Century Broadside of Prices from the Crolius Pottery. Online at https://repository.duke.edu/dc/broadsides/bdsny11271 (It is dated ca. 1820 in pencil on the document but the Crolius pottery had moved from this location ca. 1814).

African Burial Ground in New York City. Artifacts found at the site included over 22,200 salt-glazed stoneware kiln waster sherds and more than 34,000 pieces of kiln furniture and debris (Janowitz and Cheek 2009, Janowitz 2009). Before excavations started, archaeologists had speculated that kiln wasters might be found because 18th-century maps showed potteries on the edges of the "Negroes Burial Ground," as it was called at the time, on Pott Baker's Hill. The potters, members of the Crolius and Remmey families working there since the 1720s, were well known and their late-18th- and early-19th-century vessels were prized by collectors and studied by ceramic historians. Crolius potters worked in Manhattan until the 1840s. Remmey potters

FIGURE 2. Underfired Sherd with a GR Medallion. African
Burial Ground Collection (Photograph by John Abbott, 2006).

were in Manhattan until the early-19th century, then continued to work in Baltimore and Philadelphia until the end of that century.

Analysis of the salt-glazed stoneware vessel sherds from the site (most probably deposited before 1770 [Janowitz and Cheek 2009:138]) has shown how 18th-century vessels differed from those made by the potters' 19th-century descendants. Many of the sherds are from the most common forms made by later potters—jars, jugs, pitchers, tankards[1], and chamber pots—but other vessels are also represented. Teapots, plates, dishes, porringers, round mugs, and bowls are not common 19th-century salt-glazed stoneware forms, but sherds from such vessels were found at the Burial Ground. Sherds from plates, rimmed shallow bowls, and barber bowls were found at excavations nearby in City Hall Park (Bankoff and Loorya 2008). There are two main

reasons for the greater variety of forms made in the mid-18th century: training and background of the potters and ceramic choices available to consumers.

The first stoneware potter known to have worked in Manhattan was Georg Corcilius, who came from Nordhofen in the Westerwald region of Germany between 1718 and 1724 (Janowitz 2008). He was followed shortly thereafter by Johann Willem Crolius and Johannes Remmey, both of whom married into his family. All three men were trained in the Westerwald region's stoneware tradition and brought their skills, tools, and artistic sensibilities with them. David Gaimster's comprehensive book about German stoneware (Gaimster 1997) and German museum collections (Reineking-Von Bock 1971; Naumann 1980; Klinge 1996) illustrate what sorts of pots these men made in their native country. Eighteenth-century German potters made both

FIGURE 3. Side View of the Sherd in Figure 2 Showing the Line between the Sprigged Medallion and the Body. African Burial Ground Collection (Photograph by John Abbott, 2006).

teawares and tablewares, although in relatively small numbers compared to storage vessels and other drinking containers (round mugs and tall tankards) (Gaimster 1997:121). The first potters who came to New York made the same variety of vessels as they had in Germany, using American clay to make German forms.

The ceramic choices available to New Yorkers and other British colonials changed during the 18th century when white salt-glazed stoneware followed by cream-colored earthenware became widely available, particularly after the mid-1760s when creamware flooded the market. Creamware became ubiquitous, leaving no space for locally made stonewares on dinner or tea tables. By the turn of the century, American stoneware potters primarily made vessels for storage, sanitary uses, and drinking (Figure 1).

Decorations also differed over the years. The early German potters in New York continued to embellish at least some of their vessels in Westerwald styles. Westerwald vessels were usually decorated with incised and filled-in designs, sprigged motifs, and, occasionally, stamped patterns. Many of the motifs were elaborate, especially on drinking vessels (Maryland Archaeological Conservation Laboratory 2002; Metropolitan Museum of Art 2000-2019b). The incised or stamped motifs on early- to mid-19th-century American stonewares, when present, are fairly simple and sprigged designs are very rare, so archaeologists and others have reasoned that any 18th-century excavated or curated vessels or sherds found in North America that have elaborate motifs or sprigged designs came from Germany. This reasoning has been overturned by sherds excavated at the African Burial Ground.

FIGURE 4. Tankard Sherd with Reeding and Incised Decoration Filled-In with Blue and Purple. African Burial Ground Collection (Photograph by John Abbott, 2006).

FIGURE 5. Incised and Filled-In Sherds from Tankards. African Burial Ground Collection (Photograph by John Abbott, 2006).

3).[3] The GR sherds are definitely wasters: they are severely under fired and lack salt glaze, evidence of the less than optimal firing conditions of wood-fired kilns. Other waster sherds from the site have Westerwald-style incised and filled-in motifs (Figures 4 and 5). Some of the sherds have purple as well as blue coloring, a feature very rarely found on later American vessels but not uncommon on German ones.

So how can salt-glazed stoneware sherds from 18th-century assemblages be identified as German or American? Visually, the American sherds are often a duller gray or gray/buff color, particularly in cross-sections, while German sherds are almost always bright gray and are often thinner bodied. The cobalt blue on German vessels is usually brighter and clearer and decorations are more elaborate with greater use of cobalt not only in incised motifs but also as a covering for part or all of a vessel. These characteristics, however, are subjective and require a familiarity with both types of wares. X-ray fluorescence (XRF) analysis that measures trace elements in clays is a promising tool (Bernstein et al. 2016). A preliminary analysis done at Brooklyn College that compared sherds from Germany, the City Hall excavations, and vessels owned by a private collector suggested that German and American clays can be distinguished by the ratios of strontium and rubidium in their bodies: in the New York City pieces, rubidium is higher relative to strontium, while the German pieces appear to have the opposite ratio (Bankoff et al 2011). More research is needed, but meanwhile we should not assume that all the 18th-century grey stoneware sherds we excavate come from German vessels.

One very popular motif used by the Westerwald potters for trade to England was a GR medallion on mugs and tankards. The initials "GR," for George I, II or III of England, surrounded by a variety of motifs were made in small sprig molds and attached to vessels.[2] All GR decorated sherds found in North America have been attributed to Germany but they were also made in New York, based on the presence of waster sherds in the Burial Ground assemblage (Figures 2 and

META F. JANOWITZ

School of Visual Arts
89 Moraine Rd.
Morris Plains, NJ 07950, USA

References

Bankoff, Arthur H., and Alyssa Loorya (editors)
2008 The History and Archaeology of City Hall Park. Report to the New York City Department of Parks and Recreation, Flushing Meadows-Corona Park, NY, from the Brooklyn College Archaeological Research Center, Brooklyn College, CUNY, Brooklyn, NY <http://s-media.nyc.gov/agencies/lpc/arch_reports/1046_A.pdf>. Accessed 11 August 2019.

Bankoff, Arthur, Zhongqi Cheng, and Meta F. Janowitz
2011 Feasibility of Stoneware Provenance with Portable XRF Spectrometry. NEH Start Up Grant Proposal, Level II.

Barber, Edwin Atlee
1893 Pottery and Porcelain of the United States. G.P. Putnam's Sons, New York, NY. Also Google Books <https://play.google.com/books/reader?id=SJcKAAAAYAAJ&printsec=frontcover&pg=GBS.PR1>. Accessed 11 August 2019.

1903 Tulip ware of the Pennsylvania-German Potters: An Historical Sketch of the Art of Slip-Decoration in the United States. Pennsylvania Museum and School of Industrial Art, Philadelphia, PA. Also Google Books <https://play.google.com/books/reader?id=F-kCAAAAYAAJ&printsec=frontcover&output=reader&hl=en&pg=GBS.PA115>. Accessed 11 August 2019.

1904 Marks of American Potters. Trenton Historical Society, Trenton, NJ. <http://trentonhistory.org/Made/Marks.html>. Accessed 11 August 2019.

Bernstein, Johanna R., Arthur F. Goldberg, and Jennifer Mass
2016 A Comparative Scientific Study of James Morgan and the Kemple Family Stoneware. In Ceramics in America 2016, Robert Hunter, editor, pp. 220–225. Chipstone Foundation, Milwaukee, WI. <http://www.chipstone.org/article.php/748/Ceramics-in-America-2016-A-ComparativeScientific-Study-of-James-Morgan-and-the-Kemple-Family-Stoneware>. Accessed 11 August 2019.

British Pathé
1958 The Making of Wedgwood, Part I. Youtube video <https://www.youtube.com/watch?v=DDDBQh8YpfA>. Accessed 11 August 2019.

Cheek, Charles D. and Daniel G. Roberts (editors)
2009a The Archaeology of 290 Broadway Volume 1: The Secular Use of Lower Manhattan's African Burial Ground. Report to Jacobs Edwards and Kelcey, Morristown, NJ and U.S. General Services Administration, Public Buildings Service, Northeast and Caribbean Region, New York, NY, from John Milner Associates, Inc., West Chester, PA <https://www.gsa.gov/cdnstatic/largedocs/Volume_I_290Broadway.pdf>. Accessed 11 August 2019.

2009b The Archaeology of 290 Broadway Volume II: Archaeological and Historical Data Analyses. Report to Jacobs Edwards and Kelcey, Morristown, NJ and U.S. General Services Administration, Public Buildings Service, Northeast and Caribbean Region, New York, NY, from John Milner Associates, Inc., West Chester, PA <https://www.gsa.gov/cdnstatic/largedocs/Volume_II_290Broadway.pdf>. Accessed 11 August 2019.

Gaimster, David
1997 German Stoneware 1200 – 1900: Archaeology and Cultural History. British Museum Press, London, UK.

Goldberg, Arthur F., Peter Warwick, and Leslie Warwick
2008 The Eighteenth-Century New Jersey Stoneware Potteries of Captain James Morgan and the Kemple Family. In Ceramics in America 2008, Robert Hunter, editor, pp. 2–40. Chipstone Foundation, Milwaukee, WI <http://www.chipstone.org/article.php/411/Ceramics-in-America-2008/The-Eighteenth-Century-New-Jersey-Stoneware-Potteries-of-Captain-James-Morgan-and-the-Kemple-Family>. Accessed 11 August 2019.

Hunter, Robert
2014 Specializing in the Diverse: A Journey in Ten Ceramic Objects. In Ceramics in America 2014, Robert Hunter, editor, pp. 169–187. Chipstone Foundation, Milwaukee, WI <http://www.chipstone.org/article.php/697/Ceramics-in-America-2014/Specializing-in-the-Diverse:-A-Journey-in-Ten-Ceramic-Objects>. Accessed 11 August 2019.

Janowitz, Meta F.
2008 New York City Stonewares from the African Burial Ground. In *Ceramics in America 2008*, Robert Hunter, editor, pp. 41–66. Chipstone Foundation, Milwaukee, WI <http://www.chipstone.org/article.php/412/Ceramics-in-America-2008/New-York-City-Stonewares-from-the-African-Burial-Ground>. Accessed 11 August 2019.

2009 Appendix F. Analysis of Local Stoneware and Kiln Furniture from the Grave Shafts. In *The Archaeology of the African Burial Ground, Part 1*. Perry, Warren R., Jean Howson and Barbara A. Bianco, editors, pp. 525–580. Howard University Press, Washington, DC in association with the United States General Services Administration <https://www.gsa.gov/cdnstatic/largedocs/Vol2-Part3-ArchOfNYABGAppendices.pdf>. Accessed 11 August 2019.

Janowitz Meta F., and Charles D. Cheek
2009 The New York Ceramic Industry and Its Use of the Burial Ground. In *The Archaeology of 290 Broadway Volume 1: The Secular Use of Lower Manhattan's African Burial Ground*. Charles D. Cheek and Daniel G. Roberts, editors, pp. 137–192. Report to Jacobs Edwards and Kelcey, Morristown, NJ and U.S. General Services Administration, Public Buildings Service, Northeast and Caribbean Region, New York, NY, from John Milner Associates, Inc., West Chester, PA <https://www.gsa.gov/cdnstatic/largedocs/Volume_I_290Broadway.pdf>. Accessed 11 August 2019.

Klinge, Ekkart
1996 *Duits Steengoed/German Stoneware*. Rijksmuseum, Amsterdam and Uitgeverij Waanders, b.v., Zwolle, the Netherlands.

The Metropolitan Museum of Art
2000–2019a William Crolius Inkstand <https://www.metmuseum.org/art/collection/search/1981?&searchField=All&sortBy=Relevance&ft=inkstand&offset=0&rpp=80&pos=3>. Accessed 11 August 2019.

2000–2019b On-Line Collection, Koblentz Stoneware <https://www.metmuseum.org/art/collection/search#!?perPage=20&searchField=All&sortBy=Relevance&offset=0&pageSize=0&material=Pottery&geolocation=Koblenz>. Accessed 11 August 2019.

Maryland Archaeological Conservation Laboratory
2002 Rhenish [Stoneware]. <https://apps.jefpat.maryland.gov/diagnostic/ColonialCeramics/Colonial%20Ware%20Descriptions/Rhenish.html>. Accessed 11 August 2019.

Naumann, Joachim
1980 Deutsches Steinzug des 17. - 20. Jahrhunderts. *Beiträge Zur Keramik 1*. Het Jens-Museum, Deutsches Keramikmuseum, Düsseldorf, Germany.

Perry, Warren R., Jean Howson, and Barbara A. Bianco (editors)
2009 *The Archaeology of the African Burial Ground, Part 1*. Howard University Press, Washington, D.C. <https://www.nps.gov/afbg/learn/historyculture/upload/downVol2-Part1-The-Archaeology-of-the-NYABG.pdf> and <https://www.gsa.gov/cdnstatic/largedocs/Vol2-Part1-TheArchaeologyOfTheNYABG.pdf>. Accessed 11 August 2019.

Pitkin, Albert Hastings
1917 *Early American Folk Pottery, Including the History of Bennington Pottery*. The Case, Lockwood, and Brainard Company, Hartford, CT.

Reineking-Von Bock, Gisela
1971 *Steinzeug, Katalog Des Kunstgewerbemuseums Köln*. Kunstgewerbemuseum. Cologne, Germany.

Sim, Robert J., and Arthur W. Clement
1944 The Cheesequake Potteries. *Antiques* March 1944:122–125.

Watkins, Lura Woodside
1950 *Early New England Potters and Their Wares*. Harvard University Press, Cambridge, MA.

Endnotes

[1] In German language stoneware catalogues *kruik* or *kan* is most often used for short forms of drinking vessels with round bodies and tall necks and *bierpul* or *beker* is used for straight-sided tall vessels (Reineking-Von Bock 1971; Naumann 1980; Klinge 1996,). Thus, during analysis of the Burial Ground collection, the term "mug" was used for round drinking vessels and "tankard" for tall straight-sided ones.

[2] A film made at the Wedgwood factory during the 1950s shows the process of decorating Jasperware with sprigged motifs (British Pathé 1958). Extant GR vessels show many variations in the details of their letters and surrounding designs, which, with more evidence from kiln sites, might be traceable to specific potters.

[3] An extant tankard with a GR medallion discussed in Hunter (2014) might have been made in New Jersey, rather than Manhattan, at the James Morgan Sr. pottery. James Morgan Sr. was not himself a potter but likely employed potters trained in Manhattan. It is also quite possible that Johan Pieter Kemple, a stoneware potter who came to Manhattan from the same area of Germany as Cortselius during the late 1730s and who later moved to New Jersey, could have used a GR sprig mold; he was skilled in Westerwald-style decorations, as evidenced by sherds illustrated in Goldberg et al. (2008).

A Staffordshire Jug from Buenos Aires?

Sandra Guillermo | Teresita Majewski

It is not surprising to find British ceramics, particularly those manufactured in Staffordshire, England, in archaeological contexts from around the world that date from the early 19th century into the 20th century (Figure 1). What is so interesting about these finds is what they can reveal about trade, economics, households, consumer behavior, and a variety of other topics.

Commercial relations between Great Britain and southern South America were established before Argentina became independent of Spanish domination, first through clandestine trade, but from about 1825 under more formal economic relationships that established free trade between industrial Great Britain and raw-materials-rich Argentina.

The Aduana Taylor (or Taylor Customs House) in the city of Buenos Aires was the institution responsible for controlling the entry and exit of goods in Argentina during the second half of the 19th century (Figure 2). Eventually, when Argentina became an important agro-exporting country toward the end of the 19th century, even the large size of the Taylor Customs House could not accommodate the quantities of merchandise that arrived in the city. In 1891, the original building was demolished, and the customs function was moved elsewhere in Buenos Aires.

Large amounts of sediment composed of soil and domestic remains discarded by inhabitants of Buenos Aires and brought from different parts of the city were deposited on the ruins of the demolished building to cover a 7,200 m² area. The ceramic fragments that make up the Taylor Customs House collection come from fill deposited over the remains of the building from 1891 to 1894. The collection is curated at the Instituto Nacional de Antropología y Pensamiento Latinoamericano in Buenos Aires.

Here we focus on some sherds from an earthenware jug or ewer with painted floral decoration (likely part of a toilet service) recovered from excavations led by Sandra Guillermo at the Aduana Taylor (Figures 3-5) (Guillermo 2016). The non-vitreous, white-bodied earthenware sherds

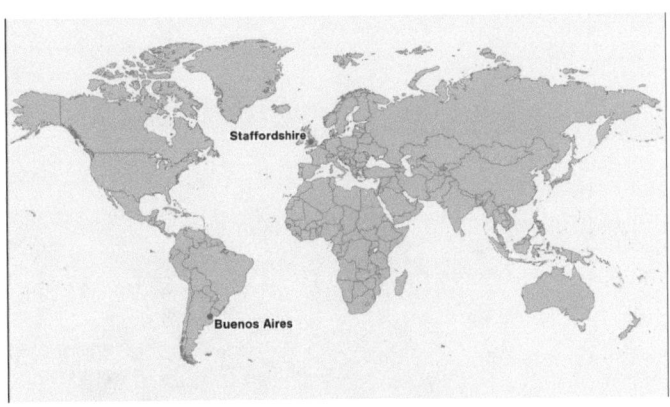

FIGURE 1. Global map showing the locations of Staffordshire, England, and Buenos Aires, Argentina (Graphic by and courtesy of Jacqueline Dominguez, 2019).

have overglaze painted (enameled) floral decoration in tan/brown, blue, and green. On the sherds associated with this vessel to date, reddish-brown lining is present around the lip and where the neck meets the body. None of the sherds bear a maker's mark. An image from the contemporary Silber & Fleming catalog provides an idea of what the complete vessel may have looked like (Figure 6) (Silber & Fleming [1880s]:67).

The sherds from the ewer or jug came from the 1891 to 1894 fill episode following demolition of the Aduana Taylor and represent domestic refuse brought in from elsewhere in Buenos Aires. The majority of the 2,500 sherds from the fill were of British origin. During initial analysis of the materials, maker's marks from the following Staffordshire potters were noted—Davenport, Copeland, Edward Walley, J & G Meakin, and Anthony Shaw. Dixon Phillips & Co., a potter from Sunderland in the northeast of England, was also represented in the collection. The manufacturer of the ewer or jug was almost certainly English, and no other similar vessels were evident in the sample.

During initial analysis of the collection, sherds representing approximately 20% of the ewer or jug were found, and it

FIGURE 2. View from the Río de la Plata of the Aduana Taylor (Taylor Customs House), Buenos Aires, Argentina (Archivo General de la Nación [Argentina], Archivo Fotográfico 47929) (Guillermo 2016:Foto No. 11).

is likely that other undecorated sherds can be matched to it as well. However, our attention was drawn to this vessel because it represents a type that is not usually found in excavations in the city. It appears to be unique in this sample and was so reminiscent of examples in the Silber & Fleming catalog, which provided a strong link to British products. Its rarity is what made us think about the contribution that these fragments can make to our knowledge of the variety of products that were acquired by residents of Buenos Aires in the 19th century. It also speaks to the extent to which residents of Buenos Aires participated in Victorian conventions regarding hygiene and personal care.

Understanding the range of vessel shapes and decoration on the ceramics recovered from the Aduana Taylor fill will help in reconstructing the nature of late-19th-century trade into Argentina from Europe. During Guillermo's preliminary analysis of the ceramics from this fill episode, she focused

on indicators on the sherds themselves that provided clues to the quality of ceramics exported to Argentina. These indicators, particularly glaze and firing flaws such as pitting, bubbling, cracking, and glaze displacements and pooling, suggest that lower-quality materials were being exported to South America.

This practice in itself is not surprising, as we know from Charles Binns' discussion in the 1907 *Manual of Practical Potting* that Argentina was a "Class III" export country to which was shipped only "the commonest china and earthenware" (Binns 1907:154–156). A tantalizing quote from the Silber & Fleming catalog (Silber & Fleming [1880s]:53) clearly indicates that wares of inferior or mixed quality could be provided to buyers: "Most of the Patterns of Toilet Services illustrated in this Catalogue can be supplied of an inferior or mixed quality, when ordered in quantities, at lower prices than quoted in our Price List. As we do not keep

Sandra Guillermo | Teresita Majewski

FIGURE 3. Painted (enameled) floral decoration on a sherd from the ewer or jug
(Photograph by Sandra Guillermo, 2018).

FIGURE 4. Close up of painted (enameled) floral decoration on a sherd from the ewer or jug
(Photograph by Sandra Guillermo, 2018).

0 cm 10

FIGURE 5. Spout, neck, and body sherds from the ewer or jug that provide clues to its shape and size (Graphic by and courtesy of Jacqueline Dominguez, 2019, from photograph by Teresita Majewski, 2018).

FIGURE 6. Illustration from the ca. 1880s Silber and Fleming catalog showing what the ewer or jug from the Aduana Taylor collection may have looked like (Silber & Fleming [1880s]:67) (Courtesy of Wordsworth Editions Ltd, Ware, Hertfordshire, UK).

these qualities in stock, two or three months are required to execute such orders."

It is likely, however, that Binns' commentary tells only part of the story. Analysis of these materials provides the first comprehensive look at a bulk sample from households that purchased what appear to be lower-quality wares. It is hoped that this investigative journey will establish links from Staffordshire factories to the South American countries, particularly Argentina. While marked examples in the Aduana Taylor collection are proof that some of the well-known Staffordshire manufacturers' products had found their way to Buenos Aires (e.g., Copeland and Davenport), initial research into documentary sources suggests that well-known and less-well-known potters had begun to venture into the potentially lucrative South American trade in the mid-to late-19th century.

The sherds from this ewer or jug hint at internal and minor aspects of the commercial relationships existing in the 19th century with southern South America. These are not yet well understood and require more in-depth study that takes into account archaeological and museum collections together with archival materials.

Sandra Guillermo | Teresita Majewski

SANDRA GUILLERMO
Ministry of Culture of the Argentine Nation
Adolfo Alsina 465, 5to. Piso, C1087AAE
Ciudad Autónoma de Buenos Aires, Argentina

TERESITA MAJEWSKI
Statistical Research, Inc.
3170 East Fort Lowell Road
Tucson, AZ 85716, USA

References

Binns, Charles
    1907 *The Manual of Practical Potting*, Revised and Enlarged Fourth Edition. Scott, Greenwood & Son, London, UK.

Guillermo, Sandra
    2016 *Arqueología Urbana*. La Aduana Taylor (1857 – 1891). Ciudad de Buenos Aires. Argentina. (Urban Archaeology: The Taylor Customs House (1857 – 1891). City of Buenos Aires. Argentina). PhotoDesign Ediciones, Cooperativa El Zócalo. Buenos Aires, Argentina.

Silber & Fleming
    [1880s] *The Silber & Fleming Glass and China Book*. Wordsworth Editions, Ware, UK. From facsimile dated 1990.

One Ordinary Extraordinary Brick

Joan H. Geismar

Let me be perfectly clear: I don't keep artifacts from archaeological sites. However, the small, ordinary, misshapen, Dutch brick in question is the exception, and I treasure it. It apparently served to help sink a 100-foot, derelict merchant vessel discovered at the 175 Water Street Site in Lower Manhattan (Figure 1), and was one of many about to be trashed (Figure 2). While "ordinary," it was totally unexpected as was the ship repurposed as cribbing to keep the landfill in while keeping the East River out.

Beginning in the late 1730s, the site was one of numerous Lower Manhattan blocks reclaimed from the East River (Figure 3). Situated between Water and Front Streets, its western boundary was Fletcher Street, and its eastern boundary John Street, initially known as Burling Slip. The middle of the block between Fletcher and John Street was our focus. It was here that we hoped to learn about many aspects of mid- to late-18th- and 19th-century life in New York City, in addition to how the block was created by its water lot grantees, mainly the city's merchant elite (one of them a woman, but that's another story).

Archaeologists investigating these Lower Manhattan landfill sites in the 1980s have referred to that decade as the "Golden Age" of New York City archaeology. It was a time when a spate of new office buildings in or near Manhattan's landmarked Seaport District often warranted archaeological investigation. The construction offered the opportunity to learn how New York City's British colonials created land from the river and changed the configuration of Manhattan.

With my degree in hand, the Soil Systems Division of Professional Services Industries, Inc., hired me as the project's Principal Investigator. On October 28, 1981, the investigation began by transforming what had been a parking lot for over 25 years (Figure 4) into an archaeological site. This meant exposing the block's backyards to locate features that included privy pits and cisterns (Figure 5). And we hit the jackpot.

Over the next three months, field archaeologists, lab technicians, specialists, and consultants exposed, recorded,

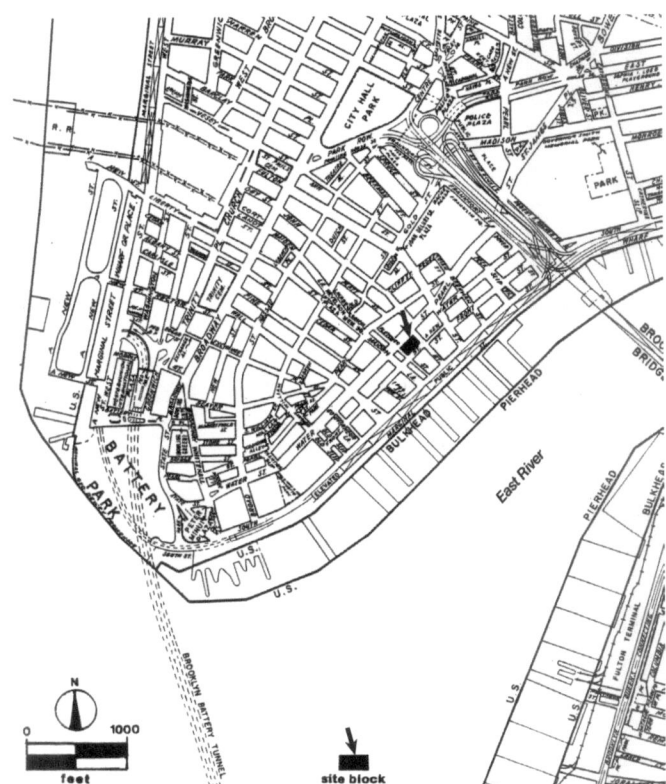

FIGURE 1. The 175 Water Street Block Location in Lower Manhattan.

and analyzed features in and material from the backyards of mixed-use structures, all but one covered by building extensions. Under these extensions were the sought-after features with their detritus from "stores" (warehouses) and domestic households. And beneath all this was the landfill; that is, the trash and soil used to fill the block structured by the parallel and perpendicular wharves required by water lot grants. These massive structures supported the streets that defined blocks and, initially, created slips (here, Burling Slip) to accommodate the merchant ships that brought goods to the water lot owners.

But the backyard features weren't our only interest. The landfill itself, and what preceded it, that is, the material

FIGURE 2. Five of the many small, misshapen yellow Dutch bricks recovered in and around the hull of *The Ronson* (Photo courtesy of Professional Service Industries, Inc., Soil Systems Division).

associated with piers, wharves, and the river bottom were also important to study. We excavated "deeptests" to determine the depth and components of the landfill.

The deeptests were excavated with a backhoe (as, of course, was much of the site clearing and removal of the backyard building extensions). Here, sampling was accomplished by excavating approximately 1 ft. levels and recovering and wet screening seven 5-gallon buckets of material from each level.

Four deeptests were excavated, the fourth and last (DT 33) near Front Street. It was here that I thought we would find the block's deepest landfill since it was the most southerly of the four and therefore the furthest into the river (in retrospect, this was not necessarily so since the depth of the landfill undoubtedly fluctuated as did the river bottom).

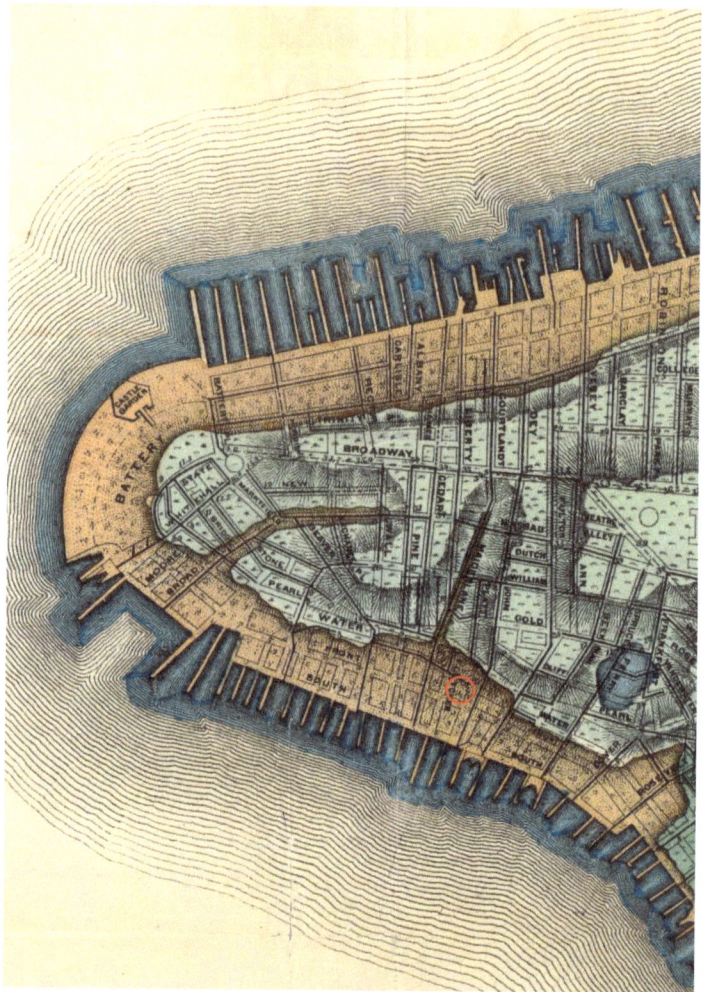

FIGURE 3. The 175 Water Street block (red circle) on Egbert L. Viele's 1865 reconstruction of Manhattan landfill (detail). The original landmass is green and the landfill is orange.

Now for the exciting part: the backhoe operator asked where to locate this final deeptest and I pointed, somewhat arbitrarily, I admit. The spot was quite far south but not where it could possibly undermine the site's construction fence on Front Street.

Joan H. Geismar

FIGURE 4. The 175 Water Street block, a parking lot, shortly before it became an archaeological site (Photo by A. Donadeo). The view is looking west toward Fletcher Street. Water Street is to the right and Front Street to the left. John Street (originally Burling Slip), which would be in the foreground, is not shown.

Being an accommodating fellow, and actually a dream of a backhoe operator, one with a delicate touch (he would pick up a bottle and lay it at my feet, intact), he began to excavate. We collected our seven bucket samples and kept digging. At about 10 ft. below the surface, the dirt fell away, exposing horizontal planks (Figure 6) and I assumed we had found the cribbing that held the landfill in place. However, as we went deeper the "cribbing" curved toward the river. In consultation with Norman Brouwer, then the maritime historian at the nearby South Street Seaport Museum, and with additional excavation, it was determined that we had serendipitously exposed the midsection, port side of the aforementioned merchant vessel incorporated into the cribbing that kept the landfill in place.

While someone said, "Joan, your ship came in," it actually heralded the end of my on-site duties at 175 Water Street. A team of nautical archaeologists from Texas A & M headed by Warren Riess and Shelli Smith was brought in to excavate a ship on land (Figure 7). The entire bow and most of the hull proved to be situated on the block (Figures 8 and 9).

FIGURE 5. The 175 Water Street block during backyard testing in early November 1981. The view is west toward Fletcher Street (Photo Courtesy of Professional Service Industries, Inc., Soil Systems Division).

FIGURE 6. Deeptest 33 after the soil had fallen away to expose what proved to be the mid-section of the port side of a derelict merchant vessel incorporated into the block's cribbing (Photo Courtesy of Professional Service Industries, Inc., Soil Systems Division). Note the gun port (arrow).

Joan H. Geismar

FIGURE 7. Excavating *The Ronson* (Photo courtesy of Professional Service Industries, Inc., Soil Systems Division).

FIGURE 8. The exposed bow of *The Ronson* covered with salt hay to prevent freezing during 1982's record breaking cold January (Photograph by author).

Initially dubbed *The Ronson* after the site's developer who was waiting in the wings to build his 32-story office tower, the ship now has a proper name. After three and a half decades, Warren Riess believes he has identified the vessel as *The Princess Carolina* constructed in the Chesapeake in 1717.

And now back to my extraordinary ordinary brick.

The ship mainly proved to contain the same artifact-laden matrix found throughout the block. The nautical archaeologists (now joined by some of the land archaeologists who had worked with me) removed, measured, and photographed

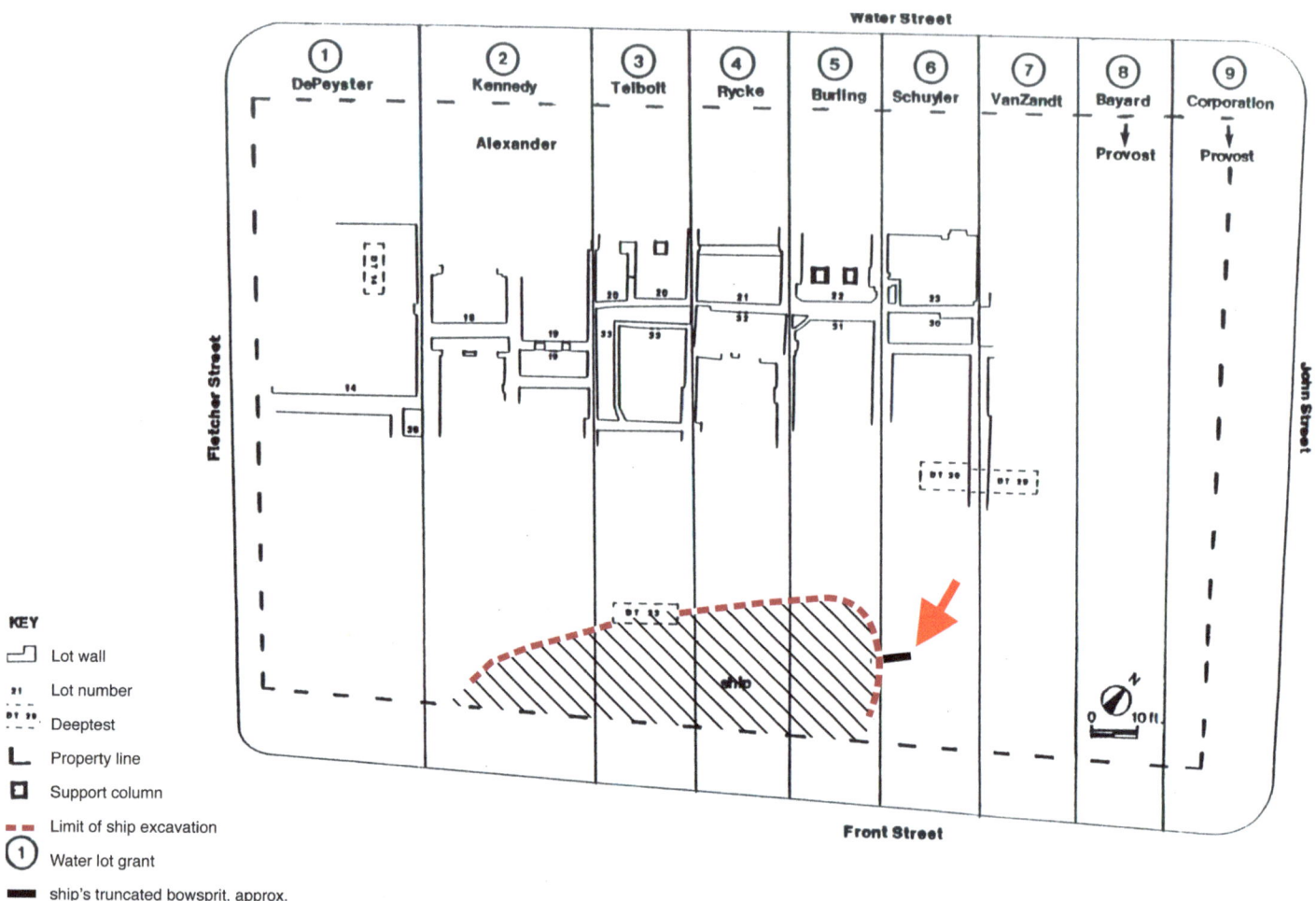

KEY

⌐┘ Lot wall

₃₁ Lot number

DT ₃₉ Deeptest

L Property line

◻ Support column

▬ ▬ ▬ Limit of ship excavation

① Water lot grant

▬▬ ship's truncated bowsprit. approx.

FIGURE 9. The 175 Water Street Excavation Plan Showing the Block's Nine Water Lots, the Water Lot Grantees, and the location of *The Ronson*. Note: the ship's bowsprit (arrow) extends into Lot 6 owned by a woman grantee (Ann Elizabeth Schuyler).

each accessible plank before it was carted off to what was then an active landfill on Staten Island. However one ship-related find was the small, misshapen bricks found in and around the vessel, apparently a component of ballast then reused to sink the vessel. These, too, were documented. When they, like the ship's planks, were about to go off to the landfill, someone asked if I would like one (or even more). With only a moment's hesitation, I said, "yes" and kept what to anyone else might be one ordinary brick. To me, not only wasn't it ordinary, but the fact that I kept it was extraordinary.

84

Joan H. Geismar

JOAN H. GEISMAR

Joan H. Geismar, Ph.D., LLC.
40 E. 83rd Street, 2E
New York, NY 10028, USA

References

Geismar, Joan H.
    1983. The Archaeological Investigation of the 175 Water Street Block, New York City, Report to HRO International, New York, NY, from Professional Service Industries, Inc., Soil Systems Division, Marietta, GA. Joan H. Geismar, Principal Investigator. (Available On-line, NYC Landmarks Preservation Commission Archaeological Reports Archive).

Viele, Egbert L.
    1865. *Sanitary and Topographical Map of the City and Island of New York.* Ferd. Mayer & Co., Lithographer, 96 Fulton Street, New York.

Endnotes

[1] Information about 175 Water Street mainly is from memory augmented by the project report (Geismar 1983).

www.ingramcontent.com/pod-product-compliance
Lightning Source LLC
Chambersburg PA
CBHW041457120626
46547CB00003B/458